RJ STARR

The Psychology of Modern Inadequacy

Why You Always Feel Behind—and What That Feeling Is Really Trying to Tell You

First edition

This book was professionally typeset on Reedsy.
Find out more at reedsy.com

For anyone who ever looked around and thought,
"Everyone else seems to know what they're doing but me."
You're not behind.
You're just awake.

"The trouble with the rat race is that even if you win, you're still a rat."

—Lily Tomlin

Contents

Preface

I didn't set out to write this book. Not really.

What I set out to do—over and over again, across lecture halls, podcast episodes, late-night conversations, and half-formed essays—was try to answer a quieter question: Why do so many people feel like they're failing at life, even when they're doing everything they were told to do?

Students come to my office with straight A's and stomach ulcers. Executives call it imposter syndrome when really, they're exhausted from shape-shifting. Caregivers say they feel "lazy" if they rest. Artists whisper about the guilt of not producing. And across almost every demographic, I hear some version of the same phrase:

"I just thought I'd be farther along by now."

That sentence stayed with me. I started writing this book to chase it down—not to correct it, but to understand the emotional architecture beneath it. What creates that sense of being perpetually behind? What internal scripts, external systems, and inherited messages form that persistent belief that who we are is not enough?

This is not a book about self-improvement. It's not another manual on how to "level up," "get motivated," or "optimize your mindset." God knows we've had enough of those. This is a book about noticing the water we're swimming in—the cultural, familial, and psychological conditions that normalize burnout, perfectionism, comparison, and shame as if they're just part of being a functioning adult.

They're not. They're part of a performance.

And many people are ready to stop performing. They just don't know what that looks like.

I wrote this book for my students, first and foremost. Many of them are navigating adulthood with the quiet fear that they're somehow doing it wrong. They're thoughtful, passionate, wildly intelligent—and still plagued by the feeling that they're lagging behind some invisible curve. They're chasing degrees and approval and TikTok algorithms while wondering why rest makes them anxious and productivity feels like oxygen.

They've been handed a culture that treats the body as a machine, the mind as a tool, and the self as a brand. And then they're told to "find balance."

This book is my attempt to tell them the truth: the problem is not who you are. It's what you've been asked to become in order to be considered valid.

But I didn't write this book *only* for students. I wrote it for the colleague who keeps achieving and still feels empty. For the parent who looks around and wonders if everyone else got the manual. For the friend who can't name what's wrong, just that they're tired down to the bone and don't know how to stop striving.

And maybe I wrote it for myself, too. For the younger version of me who thought the answer to discomfort was to work harder. Who thought self-worth could be earned through output. Who feared slowing down because it felt like failure. Who mistook hyper-productivity for being okay.

I know what it's like to hit every external milestone and still feel like you're waiting for something. For the internal permission to exhale. For someone to say, "You don't have to keep proving yourself. You're allowed to be here, as you are."

If that voice never arrived for you, let this book be that voice.

Not a lecture. Not a fix. Just a voice that says: *You're not broken. You're responding logically to an emotionally illogical world.*

Throughout this book, you'll find psychological theory woven into lived experience. That's by design. I'm not interested in presenting a sterile, abstract version of emotional struggle. I want you to see the links between trauma and perfectionism. Between attachment and burnout. Between social media and the nervous system. Between capitalism and your inner critic.

But more than anything, I want you to walk away with language.

Because when people can name what's happening inside them, they stop blaming themselves for it. When we can trace the roots of shame, fear, and comparison back to the systems that seeded them, we create room for self-compassion—not just as a technique, but as a worldview.

Some of what's in this book will feel validating. Other parts might feel disruptive. That's good. That means it's working.

The chapters are designed to hold you as you unpack some of the stories you didn't know you'd inherited. Stories about what it means to be good, successful, likable, desirable, competent. Stories about why you push yourself so hard, even when you're falling apart. Stories about who you had to become to feel safe—and what it might mean to soften out of that version.

Each chapter begins with a sensation—an emotional cue we've been taught to interpret as personal failure. Feeling behind. Feeling tired. Feeling lazy. Feeling unmotivated. Feeling like no matter how much you do, you're still not enough. From there, we dive into the psychology beneath it: what shaped that belief, and what it might mean to challenge it.

But I want to be clear: this isn't a blueprint for fixing your life. It's an invitation to stop assuming you need fixing.

You won't find five-step plans or daily habits guaranteed to rewire your brain. What you'll find instead are questions. Reflections. Psychological framing that helps you hold your experience with more gentleness. Stories that make it easier to breathe.

This book is not about transcending your humanity. It's about reclaiming it.

It's for the part of you that is exhausted by the performance of adequacy. The part that wants to stop editing yourself. The part that doesn't want to spend one more year chasing a finish line that moves every time you get close.

We live in a world that teaches us to treat adequacy like a subscription service—something that has to be renewed monthly through achievement, compliance, and relentless positivity. This book is a refusal of that model.

It's a declaration that being human is not a problem to solve.

There's a deeper truth I hope you absorb as you read: inadequacy is not the same as humanity. But when you live in a culture that profits off your insecurity, it can be hard to tell the difference.

So much of what we pathologize—procrastination, overthinking, emotional sensitivity, struggle with rest—is actually protective. It's how our nervous systems respond to past experiences, social conditioning, and invisible stressors. What we think of as "flaws" are often adaptations. They're clues.

When you begin to see that, you stop asking "What's wrong with me?" and start asking "What happened? What's being repeated here? What needs care, not critique?"

That's the shift. From pathology to pattern. From self-punishment to curiosity.

I want this book to make you curious about your life—not critical of it.

I want you to walk away with a deeper ability to sit with discomfort without spiraling into judgment. I want you to recognize the voice of your inner critic without confusing it for the truth. I want you to rest without apology. To choose presence over performance. To reclaim the parts of you that were hidden beneath the need to be impressive.

And if nothing else, I want you to feel less alone.

Because the thing about modern inadequacy is that it convinces you you're the only one feeling it. But you're not. It's everywhere. It's the quiet hum underneath ambition, the panic beneath procrastination, the ache behind overachievement. And most people are too busy pretending to admit that they're drowning.

This book is not about pretending.

It's about noticing. Noticing the water. Noticing the pressure. Noticing your body's wisdom. Noticing how many things you've already survived, and how many strategies you've used just to get here. Noticing the ways you've tried to stay lovable in systems that don't know how to love complexity.

I don't believe you need a complete transformation. I believe you need more room. More grace. More options.

More models of what it looks like to be human—and still enough.

And that's what I hope this book gives you.

A different mirror. A different voice. A different set of questions to sit with in the quiet moments when everything feels like too much and not enough, all at once.

May it remind you that you are not behind. You are not failing. You are not a broken project in need of constant fixing.

You are a person. Still becoming. Still worthy.
And still allowed to live a life that doesn't need to be earned.

-RJ

* * *

Introduction

You're Not Broken. You're Just Trying to Keep Up.

There's a specific kind of ache that follows you through modern life. It's not always loud, but it's consistent. You wake up and feel it before your feet hit the ground. A sense of being behind—behind in your career, behind in your healing, behind where you should be in life. Even when you've accomplished something, it never seems like enough. Even when you're doing your best, some part of you still whispers that you should be doing more.

That feeling has a name. It's inadequacy. And in this moment in history, it isn't a personal problem—it's a widespread psychological condition. One that almost no one talks about directly, but almost everyone carries.

The people who feel this way the most are often the ones doing the hardest emotional work. The ones showing up, striving, healing, helping, creating, surviving. Ironically, it's not usually the arrogant or detached who feel inadequate. It's the conscientious. The thoughtful. The people trying to get life right.

We've been conditioned to believe that if we feel inadequate, something must be wrong *with us*. We're told to try harder, fix ourselves, stay positive, lean in, hustle. But the truth is more uncomfortable—and more liberating. The truth is that you've been trained to feel inadequate. Not because you are. But because it keeps you striving, comparing, and proving. And that serves a culture built around achievement, consumption, and emotional control.

This book is not about teaching you how to feel like enough. That would be another impossible standard—another way to evaluate whether you're "doing healing right." What I want instead is to help you understand the systems and stories that made you question your enough-ness in the first place.

Inadequacy isn't random. It has psychological roots. It starts in the way we're taught to earn love. It deepens when worth is tied to performance. It flourishes in cultures of constant comparison and disappears only when we realize it was never a reflection of our truth—it was a consequence of our training.

You're not the only one who feels this way. I've worked in classrooms, listened to thousands of people across platforms, and studied the emotional patterns that shape how we live. What I've learned is this: modern inadequacy is not a diagnosis. It's a default setting. And we can change it—but only by understanding what it really is.

This is a book about the inner architecture of your self-evaluation. It's about shame, perfectionism, burnout, resistance, motivation, identity, trauma, and cultural pressure. It's about the hidden emotional economy that rewards your exhaustion and punishes your pauses. And most of all, it's about learning how to locate your worth without having to constantly prove it.

In the pages ahead, I'm going to walk you through how this feeling of "not enough" gets installed, how it shows up in everyday life, and what's required to reclaim a version of self-worth that isn't built on depletion or performance.

Some of what you read will feel uncomfortably familiar. Some of it will feel like relief. My job is not to push you toward self-optimization. It's to offer clarity—to give you language for what you've always felt but maybe never had permission to name.

This isn't a feel-good book. It's a feel-real one. It's not about blame or self-esteem tips or rewiring your brain overnight. It's about understanding the psychological system you've been living inside—and what it takes to start relating to yourself in a way that doesn't rely on constant repair.

If you're reading this, I already know one thing about you: you're trying. Maybe harder than anyone knows. And that effort deserves more than silence. It deserves recognition, language, and the kind of insight that doesn't ask you to be a different person, but allows you to *finally come home* to who you already are.

Let's begin.

1

Where the Feeling Begins

Understanding the Emotional Blueprint

Before we ever had jobs, relationships, or bank accounts—before there were resumes or timelines or social media feeds—we had a sense of self forming quietly inside us. That self was shaped not by who we really were, but by how the world responded to us. Approval. Disapproval. Attention. Neglect. Encouragement. Correction. We were absorbing it all, long before we had language for any of it. And somewhere in that invisible learning process, a template began to form—one that would shape how we saw ourselves for decades to come.

This chapter is about that template.

Inadequacy doesn't begin in adulthood. It's not the product of just one bad relationship, one failure, one disappointing job. It starts earlier. Much earlier. It starts when we begin to associate our emotional survival with being liked, praised, obedient, or high-achieving. It starts when our worth becomes a negotiation instead of a given.

The language of inadequacy is learned. And like any language, we pick it up most fluently when we're young, when our nervous systems are still developing, and when we depend on others to interpret our value back to us. That means the first time we felt "not enough" wasn't a dramatic moment. It was subtle. Maybe even invisible. But it was powerful enough to sink its way into how we think, how we relate, and how we measure ourselves now.

In the sections ahead, we'll trace this back to its origins—not to assign blame, but to illuminate the architecture. Shame doesn't build itself. The inner critic doesn't appear out of nowhere. The fear of being behind doesn't just show up because you're scrolling Instagram too much. These patterns have history. And understanding that history is the first step toward changing the relationship you have with yourself.

We'll begin with the quietest part of it all: the way love and shame became linked, and how "being enough" turned into something you had to earn.

The Quiet Origins of Shame

Shame doesn't usually begin in fire. It begins in subtlety. It begins in the tone of someone's voice when you speak out of turn. In the moment a caregiver shifts their face in response to your tears. In the pattern of being praised only when you're useful. It shows up when your joy is too loud, your sadness too inconvenient, or your questions too complicated for the adults around you to handle. And because children are built to survive before they are built to understand, we absorb these cues not as information—but as truth.

It's easy to believe shame is always loud and shattering, that it must come from cruelty or abuse. But some of the deepest shame is born inside environments that were structured by love but shaped by fragility. Parents who meant well but couldn't regulate. Teachers who encouraged you while also quietly demanding perfection. Extended family members who offered warmth as long as you didn't disrupt the emotional balance of the room. Shame thrives in these spaces not because they're overtly hostile, but because they quietly teach you that your emotional existence must be edited for the comfort of others.

By the time we can form full sentences, many of us have already learned that there is a difference between being loved and being accepted. Being loved might still come with conditions. Being accepted—fully, without performance—was rarely modeled. And so we learn to adapt. We suppress what's messy. We amplify what pleases. And slowly, a pattern is set: my worth is directly related to how well I can avoid upsetting others.

This is the beginning of the emotional blueprint. Not the part we talk about in therapy right away, and not the part most people recognize when they feel "not good enough." But it's where the seed gets planted. Not in catastrophe, but in the repetition of small, subtle transactions. Do well, and you're safe. Fall short, and you're met with discomfort. So we start performing. And that performance starts to feel like our personality.

If someone praised you often for being "mature," "well-behaved," "so responsible," or "such a good helper," you may have mistaken those qualities for your identity. But often, those labels aren't reflections of who you truly were—they're reflections of how you made other people's lives easier. And while that's not inherently harmful, it becomes a breeding ground for shame when it teaches you to equate your goodness with your usefulness.

It's not always what was said to us that formed the foundation of shame. It's what was implied. You may have been told you were loved no matter what. But if the people around you tensed when you cried, rushed to fix you when you were upset, or praised you most when you were high-functioning, the message became clear: don't just be. Be useful. Be manageable. Be exceptional. Be emotionally efficient.

That kind of messaging doesn't create resilience. It creates anxiety. And it wires a person to believe that their value is contingent on how little trouble they cause. Shame, then, becomes a kind of preemptive emotional labor. You start rehearsing how to be before you even enter a room. You start evaluating your words before you speak. You begin thinking not in terms of what you need, but in terms of what will keep everyone around you comfortable. And when you inevitably fall short of that impossible standard, shame is there—whispering that your messiness is proof of your unworthiness.

Most people don't recognize this as shame. They call it self-awareness. Or responsibility. Or high standards. But shame is rarely that honest. It likes to disguise itself as something noble. It tells you that your critical inner voice is just "keeping you sharp." It tells you that your fear of slowing down is just "motivation." It tells you that your reluctance to ask for help is just a sign of your independence. And we believe it, because by the time we're old enough to question it, it already sounds like our own voice.

The problem is, when you grow up associating emotional safety with performance, you never learn how to feel safe just existing. You never learn how to be held in your fullness—only in your polished form. And so you begin to manage yourself as though you are a brand. You curate, repress, and perform. Not because you're fake. But because somewhere deep inside, you still believe that being fully seen would be too much for someone to handle.

This kind of shame doesn't just affect how we see ourselves. It shapes our relationships, our goals, our sense of time. People who carry this early shame often become either overachievers or underfunctioners, perfectionists or people-pleasers, emotionally distant or chronically apologetic. Some swing between extremes. But the underlying pattern remains: they're never quite convinced they're doing life right.

And so they seek confirmation—more credentials, more affirmation, more reassurance, more control. They read more books, try harder in therapy, take more courses, fine-tune their diets, optimize their mornings, and search endlessly for the version of themselves that will finally feel like enough. They do this not because they are shallow, but because they are desperate to feel internally whole in a world that taught them their wholeness had to be proven.

And yet, even as they succeed, even as they "do the work," the feeling of being behind lingers. Because the blueprint underneath hasn't changed. They still carry the early belief that love is a reward, not a right. That worth must be renewed constantly. That rest must be earned. That the deeper parts of themselves are only welcome once they're cleaned up, healed, or made useful.

We don't talk enough about how exhausting this is. To live with a quiet panic that you're not doing enough. To walk through life in emotional performance mode. To feel like you've spent your entire existence trying to be lovable in the right way—and still don't feel safe. That is the inheritance of shame that was never named. And it is more common than most people realize.

There is no shame in shame. There is only the question of what happens when we finally see it for what it is—not a personal flaw, not a moral weakness, not a personality trait—but a learned emotional response to a world that made us earn our place.

The work begins when we recognize that we were never supposed to feel this way. That we were not meant to live in constant self-evaluation. That our feelings are not a problem to be solved, but messages to be understood. And that our enough-ness was never supposed to be up for debate.

That debate began a long time ago. Not because we were broken. But because we were human, trying to make sense of the world using the only tools we had. That understanding doesn't erase the shame. But it gives us a way to begin unlearning it.

When love becomes conditional early in life, we learn to perform. But when we begin to understand where that performance came from, we give ourselves the first real chance to stop. To listen. To be seen. And, maybe for the first time, to belong—to ourselves—without having to earn it.

Performance-Based Worth

By the time many of us reached adolescence, our identities were already entangled with our achievements. We were the kids who got praised for our grades, our manners, our talent, our initiative. At first, the recognition felt good—like confirmation that we were doing something right. But beneath the surface, something else was happening. The praise wasn't just encouragement. It was instruction. And it was quietly teaching us that our worthiness was conditional.

When a child is consistently rewarded for performance—whether it's academic, emotional, or behavioral—something essential begins to shift. We stop asking *Who am I?* and start asking *What do people like about me?* Then we chase that version. We learn quickly that being exceptional gets more attention than being honest. That being mature earns more approval than being messy. That being agreeable creates more safety than being real.

And once that link is formed—between external praise and internal safety—it's very difficult to break. It becomes the basis for a way of being in the world that is externally oriented but internally fragile. A way of moving through life that looks successful from the outside, but often feels hollow, anxious, or precarious underneath.

The roots of performance-based worth usually don't start with overt pressure. In fact, they often come from the very people who said all the right things. You're enough. We love you no matter what. Just do your best. But children don't learn by words alone. They learn by rhythm. By what's repeated. By what lights up their caregivers' faces. By what gets them connection. And over time, the child begins to associate their value with the version of themselves that makes life easier for the people they depend on.

Maybe you were the high achiever, always trying to stay ahead. Maybe you were the peacemaker, always smoothing things over. Maybe you were the "old soul," carrying emotional responsibility far beyond your years. However it looked, the message was the same: your worth is in what you do, not who you are.

And here's the deeper cost—when you build an identity around performance, you lose access to your internal self. You become what others reflect back to you. You build habits of excellence, empathy, problem-solving, leadership—but you also build a nervous system that's calibrated to external cues. You learn to anticipate what others need before they ask. You try to stay two steps ahead of disappointment. You scan the room before speaking. You strive for constant improvement, not because you're greedy for growth, but because standing still feels dangerous.

Many of the highest-functioning adults I've worked with carry this exact pattern. They're articulate, capable, over-responsible. They're the go-to person in a crisis. They're the ones everyone assumes are doing just fine. But underneath, they're tired in a way that sleep doesn't fix. Because they're still living inside the emotional economy they learned in childhood—where their worth must be constantly renewed through effort.

And it's not just emotional. It becomes neurological. The brain adapts to reinforcement. If achievements are met with affection, the brain lights up. That connection between success and safety becomes hardwired. So even as adults, we chase the same hit: the grade, the compliment, the promotion, the sense of being seen. Not out of ego, but out of learned survival.

This wiring is difficult to spot, because it often leads to socially rewarded behavior. People who operate from performance-based worth often look like leaders. They are productive, organized, dependable, impressive. But they are also often deeply lonely. Because the more you perform, the harder it becomes to show the parts of yourself that aren't curated. The parts that don't sparkle. The parts that need rest. Or reassurance. Or repair.

This isn't to say that achievement is wrong. Or that being competent is a problem. The issue is when those qualities become the *only* path to self-worth. When you begin to fear that if you stop achieving, people will stop caring. That if you slow down, you'll become irrelevant. That if you disappoint someone, the entire relationship will collapse.

That's not personality. That's emotional conditioning.

And it's often invisible until something breaks. Maybe you burn out. Maybe you underperform for the first time. Maybe you start dropping balls because your nervous system just can't carry it anymore. And suddenly, the identity you've built around competence begins to wobble. You don't just feel tired. You feel fraudulent. Exposed. Unmoored.

This collapse doesn't come from weakness. It comes from years of emotional overextension. Years of managing your image. Years of showing up even when you were empty. Years of hiding the messy parts because you were never taught that love could hold them.

I've seen this play out in high-achieving students, perfectionistic professionals, eldest daughters, adult children of emotionally unpredictable parents, immigrant kids, gifted kids, former child prodigies, therapists, caretakers, and quiet over-functioners in every possible walk of life. People who spent so long being told they were exceptional that they never learned they could be held in their ordinariness. People who became fluent in emotional labor but never learned the dialect of self-permission.

And here's the paradox: the better you get at performing worthiness, the harder it is to believe you are worthy without performing. So you keep going. Even when you're exhausted. Even when you hate it. Even when no one is asking anymore. Because underneath the task list and the goals and the accolades is a simple, terrified question: *If I stop doing, who will I be?*

The tragedy of performance-based worth isn't just the burnout. It's the alienation. The distance you create between your internal experience and your external life. You can't rest because rest feels like regression. You can't speak your truth because you're afraid it will disappoint someone. You can't slow down because your nervous system has only ever known speed.

And the longer you live this way, the harder it becomes to remember that there was ever another option. That you were once a child who didn't need to earn anything. That your value wasn't supposed to be calculated. That your worth was never meant to depend on your output.

That's what performance-based worth erases: the memory of unstructured being. The safety of mess. The possibility that your presence—not your performance—could be the thing people cherish.

Reclaiming that possibility takes more than a break or a boundary. It takes grief. You have to mourn the years you spent performing. You have to acknowledge the praise that felt like pressure. You have to feel the weight of all the roles you played just to keep your place in the room. And then, slowly, you begin to build a new internal rhythm. One that doesn't hinge on doing everything right, but on trusting that your humanity is already enough.

The work isn't to stop achieving. The work is to stop tying your identity to what you achieve. To know that your tenderness, your limitations, your imperfection—those aren't liabilities. They're the places where real connection begins. And they were never meant to be hidden behind your resume.

You are not your performance. You are not your checklist. You are not your discipline, your image, or your productivity. You are the person underneath all of that—the one who has always been there, waiting to be seen not for what you can do, but for who you actually are.

Trauma, Attachment, and Evaluation

The inner critic doesn't arrive fully formed. It's built piece by piece, often in response to environments that couldn't meet us where we were emotionally. And most of the time, it forms before we even know what it's called. We learn to evaluate ourselves by the standards of the people we depended on—parents, teachers, older siblings, community figures. And if those standards were inconsistent, unpredictable, or confusing, the evaluation never stops.

It becomes internalized. It becomes the voice in your head asking if you've done enough, if you are enough, if you've earned the right to rest, speak, or just exist.

Attachment theory gives us a foundation here, but not just in the clinical sense. This isn't about diagnosing your attachment style. It's about understanding how your earliest emotional bonds taught you to assess your place in the world. If you had caregivers who were emotionally attuned, who consistently responded to your needs without making you feel like a burden, then your internal landscape likely developed with some baseline sense of security. But if that attunement was absent, inconsistent, or conditional, then your self-concept grew up in a state of vigilance.

People don't always recognize emotional inconsistency as trauma. Especially not when their basic needs were met or when their caregivers "meant well." But trauma, at its core, is not defined by what happened—it's defined by how the nervous system experienced what happened. If love felt unpredictable, if comfort had to be earned, if closeness depended on compliance, then your system adapted. And part of that adaptation was becoming hyper-aware of how you were being evaluated.

Inconsistent emotional environments don't just make us anxious. They make us strategic. A child who doesn't know which version of a parent will walk through the door becomes an expert in reading tone. A child who gets affection only after excelling becomes obsessed with achievement. A child who is punished for expressing need will learn to become invisible. These strategies are incredibly intelligent responses to emotional unpredictability. But they teach one very dangerous lesson: that safety depends on getting it right.

And getting it right is exhausting. Because the rules are always shifting. One day, your sadness might be met with softness. The next day, it might be ignored. One week, your efforts are praised. The next, they're not even acknowledged. So you start scanning. You build emotional algorithms. You read facial expressions with the precision of a trained analyst. You become fluent in managing the emotional climate of your surroundings. And in the process, you lose contact with your own.

This is how the inner evaluator is born. It starts as a defense mechanism. A way to stay safe. A way to stay needed. A way to prevent rejection, abandonment, or humiliation. And eventually, it no longer needs external input. It becomes automated. You begin evaluating yourself before anyone else can. You start pre-rejecting your own emotions, doubting your own needs, criticizing your own instincts. Not because you're harsh. But because you learned that vigilance was safer than vulnerability.

For many adults, this pattern doesn't show up as clear trauma. It shows up as self-doubt. As indecision. As over-explaining, over-apologizing, over-delivering. It shows up in the silence after sending an email and wondering if your tone was too direct. It shows up in the way you replay conversations, worried you said too much. It shows up in the fear that if someone doesn't respond with enthusiasm, you must have disappointed them.

These are not flaws. They are adaptations. They are the emotional artifacts of a nervous system that never got to fully settle. And because you were likely praised for your emotional awareness, your maturity, your thoughtfulness, you probably never stopped to question whether those traits were born from genuine wholeness or from chronic self-monitoring.

This isn't about blaming your upbringing. It's about understanding what your system had to do in order to feel safe. When caregivers are emotionally inconsistent, children don't make sense of it by thinking, "This person is unpredictable." They think, "I must be doing something wrong." And that belief gets reinforced over and over, until it becomes a core operating system. If someone is cold with you? Must be your fault. If someone withdraws? You must have pushed too hard. If someone praises you? You better make sure you stay worthy of it.

This relentless self-evaluation creates a fractured identity. On the outside, you may look grounded, successful, even confident. But on the inside, you're always checking—always questioning whether you're acceptable, lovable, or too much. And it's not because you're insecure. It's because your earliest experiences taught you that love is not something to receive—it's something to protect, perform for, and maintain.

And so even your growth becomes part of the evaluation. You don't just want to heal. You want to do it perfectly. You read the right books, go to the right workshops, follow the right voices. But even as you grow, the inner critic keeps score. You're not moving fast enough. You're not getting it right. You should be further along by now. Healing, instead of being a return to self, becomes another arena for proving yourself.

What's cruel about this cycle is that the very parts of you that learned to survive are now the parts being criticized. Your high-functioning tendencies, your people-pleasing, your avoidance, your perfectionism—these are not evidence of failure. They are evidence of strategy. Of creativity. Of adaptation. And until those parts are seen with compassion instead of judgment, the evaluation never stops.

There's a specific kind of loneliness that comes from constantly evaluating yourself. It's the loneliness of never getting to be raw, unguarded, unfiltered. It's the loneliness of wondering if anyone really knows you, or if they just know the version of you that performs well. And it's that loneliness that drives many people to keep performing—because stopping would mean risking rejection. But continuing means never being seen.

There is a way out. But it doesn't begin with fixing yourself. It begins with seeing yourself. Seeing the strategies you've used as brilliant. Seeing the anxiety as communication. Seeing the inner critic as a protector that's over-functioning. And then, slowly, learning to relate to yourself with curiosity instead of critique.

That shift—from internal judgment to internal witnessing—is not quick. It requires repetition, regulation, and reflection. But once it begins, something profound happens. The inner evaluator starts to soften. The inner child starts to feel safe. And the person you've always been—underneath the monitoring, the managing, the masking—begins to return.

Not because you've arrived at some perfect version of yourself. But because you've finally stopped treating your survival strategy as a flaw. And started recognizing it for what it always was: a sign of just how hard you worked to stay connected to love in a world that didn't always know how to offer it consistently.

The First Time You Felt Behind

It probably wasn't dramatic. That first moment you felt behind in life didn't announce itself as a crisis. It was quieter than that. Maybe it was the look someone gave you when you didn't understand something "everyone else" already seemed to get. Maybe it was when you watched a friend move ahead—academically, socially, emotionally—and something inside you contracted. Or maybe it happened slowly, over time, as the world around you kept moving and you began to feel like you were somehow not keeping pace, like you'd missed a memo that everyone else had received.

The feeling of being behind rarely begins in adulthood. By the time we reach our twenties or thirties and start naming it, the emotion is already old. It's been lurking in our nervous system for years, shaping how we interpret our progress, our value, and our identity. It may not have had language back then—but it had weight.

Children are incredibly attuned to rhythm. We know when we're out of sync, even before we know why. A kid doesn't need to be told directly that they're behind to feel it. They just have to notice how others are celebrated, how achievements are stacked, how effort is measured. And if the timing of their development—emotionally, cognitively, socially—doesn't line up with their peers, the interpretation almost always becomes personal.

I must be late.

I must be slow.

I must not be good enough.

And once that interpretation sets in, it rarely stays localized. You don't just feel behind in math class or in your reading level or on the playground. You start to feel fundamentally out of step with life itself. That feeling deepens with each new context—when you don't get picked for the team, when someone else has their first kiss before you do, when you realize you're the only one who hasn't been invited, hasn't advanced, hasn't "figured it out."

Sometimes it's tied to very real external disparities. Unequal access to resources. Learning differences that went unrecognized. Socioeconomic limitations that kept you from the same experiences your peers had. But more often than not, the emotional impact of being behind has less to do with the facts of your development and more to do with the *story* you begin to tell yourself about what that difference means.

And the story almost always centers shame.

Other people are ahead because they're better.

I'm behind because I'm flawed.

I have to catch up.

So you try. You try harder. You mimic those who seem more advanced. You look for shortcuts. You overcompensate. You pretend to understand. You reach for whatever signals success in the culture around you—grades, status, charm, compliance. And even if you eventually do "catch up" in some visible way, the emotional blueprint is already set. You carry the belief that you are perpetually behind, and now everything you do has to be faster, sharper, more polished, more efficient.

The cultural pressure doesn't help. The world rewards those who reach milestones early and treats delayed development like a character flaw. There are socially constructed timelines for everything: walking, talking, reading, dating, graduating, marrying, achieving, settling down. We've absorbed those timelines so deeply that we rarely question them. When we fall outside them—by a month, a year, a decade—we assume the problem is us.

By adolescence, the emotional pattern becomes fully internalized. Now it's not just about moments of feeling behind—it's about a general sense of not measuring up. You start comparing yourself compulsively. You interpret every delay or detour as evidence that you're failing. You become sensitive to signs of progress in others, not out of envy, but out of a desperate need to recalibrate: Am I doing life right? Am I on time?

That internal clock, once disrupted, never feels trustworthy again. And so you begin to outsource your sense of timing to others. You look at their paths to gauge your own. You use their careers, relationships, bodies, productivity, and confidence as data points. But the problem is, you're comparing your inner experience to someone else's external performance. And that comparison is never fair. It's not supposed to be.

There's another layer to this: the emotional pain of not being seen for where you actually were. Many people who felt behind as children weren't just outpaced—they were overlooked. Teachers who didn't have the bandwidth to slow down. Parents who pushed without understanding. Systems that rewarded conformity and punished difference. The feeling of being behind became tied to invisibility. You weren't just late—you were forgotten.

And so the wound becomes deeper than just comparison. It becomes about belonging. You don't just want to catch up—you want to be part of something. You want to know that you're not broken. That you're not the outlier. That you're not alone.

But that's rarely what you're told. Instead, you're given strategies. You're told to work harder, try different tools, push through, build resilience. And while some of that may help practically, it doesn't address the root wound: the shame of feeling like you were always arriving too late to matter.

As adults, that early feeling shows up in places you wouldn't expect. You might feel uneasy when others talk about their accomplishments. You might downplay your own. You might avoid trying something new unless you know you'll excel. You might fear taking up space in rooms where you assume everyone is ahead of you. And even when you succeed, it doesn't quite land. Because the metric you're using isn't external anymore—it's internalized. It's a moving finish line that keeps shifting every time you get close.

The irony is, many people who carry this feeling are anything but behind. They're often thoughtful, capable, deeply introspective. But they struggle to see themselves clearly. Because they're not measuring their growth by their actual development—they're measuring it against an invisible standard rooted in early shame.

There is no universal timeline. And yet, the pressure to be "on track" is one of the most enduring emotional burdens we carry. It starts early. It hides deep. And it affects everything—from how we approach goals to how we relate to others to how we talk to ourselves in the quietest moments of our day.

To begin healing from this, we don't need motivational speeches. We need to go back to that first moment. The moment you first felt like you were behind. The moment you absorbed that your pace was wrong. That your development was embarrassing. That your questions were too slow, too simple, too much.

And then we need to do something that didn't happen the first time: offer understanding instead of evaluation. That younger version of you didn't need to be pushed. They needed to be met. Not rushed toward "fixing," but reassured that their rhythm was still valid. Still human. Still worthy of support.

That validation didn't arrive back then. But it can arrive now. And the more we practice seeing our pace without judgment, the more we disrupt the internal timeline that was never truly ours to begin with.

Feeling behind is not a diagnosis. It's a signal. A call to reconnect with your own rhythm, your own pace, your own quiet timing. Not because you have to prove anything. But because that's where your life actually happens—in the space where you stop comparing and start returning to yourself.

* * *

2

You Should Be Farther Along by Now

It's one of the most quietly painful thoughts we carry—one that never needs to be said out loud to have power. You should be farther along by now. By this age. In your career. In your healing. In your love life. In your sense of self. There's a map in your mind, even if you never meant to draw it. And somehow, without ever consciously agreeing to it, you've come to believe that you're off-course.

This belief doesn't come from nowhere. It's been embedded in us from early on, like a cultural clock we're all expected to sync to. By a certain age, you're supposed to know who you are. Have your finances in order. Be in a healthy relationship. Have the degree, the job, the house, the internal peace. Or at least be actively working toward it. And if you're not? You must have fallen behind. Or failed. Or missed something critical along the way.

This chapter is about that hidden timeline—the one that was never formally handed to you, but has shaped the way you measure your life anyway. It's about the quiet rules that tell us when success should arrive, when healing should be done, when relationships should solidify, when meaning should emerge. It's about the false promise that if we just stay on schedule, we'll be okay.

There's nothing wrong with having goals. There's nothing wrong with caring about progress. But when those goals are driven by comparison, fear, or shame, they lose their meaning. And when progress becomes a race against an imaginary clock, we don't just lose time—we lose the ability to trust our own process.

In the sections ahead, we'll take a closer look at how the cultural calendar of success took hold, why we compare ourselves so compulsively, how visibility has distorted our sense of timing, and why the path we're all chasing may not even exist in the way we think it does.

Because the truth is, most of us aren't behind. We're just measuring our lives with someone else's ruler.

The Cultural Calendar of Success

There's a story you've been told—probably without words—about how life is supposed to unfold. It starts early. Childhood is for innocence. Your teenage years are for discovery and rebellion. Your twenties are for achievement and exploration. By your thirties, you should be building something stable. By your forties, you should be successful, secure, and maybe even wise. By your fifties, you should be harvesting the benefits of all your previous effort. And by your sixties, you should have made peace with everything that came before.

This is the cultural calendar of success. And it's as fictional as it is influential.

No one hands it to you formally. It's not written on a syllabus or handed out at graduation. But you feel it. You see it reinforced in movies, advertisements, social media feeds, family gatherings, career ladders, even in the questions strangers ask. Are you dating anyone? What do you do? When are you having kids? How long have you been at your job? The questions aren't just casual—they're chronological cues. They reinforce the idea that there's a right time for everything, and a wrong time too.

And if you miss the window? You're behind.

The pressure isn't just external. It internalizes early and lives in the body. It shows up when you feel shame for not knowing your passion yet. It surfaces when your relationship ends and you're suddenly "off-track." It lives in the panic that wakes you up at night wondering if you've wasted too much time, taken too many detours, or stayed too long in a version of your life that no longer fits.

But who decided this timeline? Who decided when you should be settled, or self-assured, or fully formed? These markers are rarely grounded in psychology, development, or even lived reality. They're built around industry. Around marketing. Around what's easiest to package and sell. Around narratives that work well on paper but fall apart in actual human lives.

The life timeline is especially punishing for those whose paths haven't followed the dominant script. For people who lost years to trauma, caretaking, poverty, illness, or systemic barriers. For people who started over—by necessity or by choice. For those who pursued meaning over money, or healing over hustle. For those whose timelines got disrupted by something they couldn't predict, control, or avoid. In other words, most of us.

And yet, even knowing all of this, the internal pressure persists. We measure ourselves not just by where we are, but by where we think we *should* be. We carry these invisible benchmarks like weight. The age by which we should have found "our person." The job title we should have reached by now. The emotional maturity we should have mastered. And when reality doesn't align with those benchmarks, we don't question the timeline. We question ourselves.

What's wrong with me?

Why am I so far behind?

How do I catch up?

The cultural calendar doesn't offer answers. It only offers judgment. And because it's so rarely examined directly, most people assume their discomfort is personal. They assume they're late, unmotivated, broken, or failing. But the real problem is not their pace—it's the map.

One of the cruelest features of the life timeline myth is that it ignores context. It doesn't care where you started. It doesn't account for the emotional cost of survival. It doesn't recognize the complexity of grief, or the weight of caregiving, or the time it takes to heal from being unseen. It treats every delay as a failure and every divergence as a deficiency.

And so people scramble. They push themselves to catch up. They rush into relationships, jobs, or commitments that look right on the outside but feel hollow on the inside. They silence the parts of themselves that are still forming, still grieving, still growing. They perform adulthood before they're ready, not out of deception, but out of fear that their real pace won't be accepted.

The timeline also gets tangled with identity. For many, being "on time" isn't just about security—it's about legitimacy. Especially in communities where being taken seriously depends on proving your competence. If you're the first in your family to go to college, the first to own a home, the first to access opportunities that others take for granted, the pressure to stay "on track" can feel like a matter of survival. Any delay feels like letting people down. Any detour feels like discrediting yourself. And the calendar becomes a source of both motivation and quiet panic.

But life doesn't happen in clean phases. It happens in loops and spirals and nonlinear returns. Some people find their calling at 19. Others at 49. Some people marry early and regret it. Others fall in love for the first time after raising children alone. Some people take years to feel safe enough to heal. Others seem to grow quickly, then collapse when they realize they've built a life around pleasing others.

There is no singular calendar. There is no universal trajectory. There is only the life you are living, and the meaning you make of it.

The real question isn't whether you're on time. It's whether your timing is *true*—whether it reflects your reality, your needs, your healing, your values. A person who takes ten extra years to become grounded is not behind. They're building something real. A person who moves slower because they're carrying trauma is not failing. They're surviving with integrity. A person who seems "late" to the game but arrives fully awake is not lost. They're exactly where they need to be.

But to live by that truth, you have to be willing to challenge the calendar. You have to be willing to grieve the milestones you didn't reach when you were "supposed to." You have to forgive the version of yourself who couldn't go faster. And you have to stop looking at your life like a timeline—and start seeing it as a path. A path with curves and setbacks and delays and miracles and moments of clarity that only come after you thought you'd already missed your chance.

You haven't missed it. You're not too late. You're not off-course. You're just not living by the cultural myth anymore.

And that, in itself, is its own kind of freedom.

Comparison as a Coping Strategy

Most of us think comparison is just a bad habit—something we're supposed to grow out of with age or perspective. We know it makes us feel worse. We know it leads to self-doubt, insecurity, jealousy, or even paralysis. But what's less obvious is why we do it so compulsively. Why, even with all the self-awareness and insight in the world, we can't seem to stop measuring ourselves against others. The truth is, comparison isn't just a reflex. It's a coping mechanism. And it's often one we learned to rely on long before we even knew what it was.

At its core, comparison is a way of seeking orientation. When the inner sense of self feels shaky, we look outward for cues. Are we doing okay? Are we behind? Are we visible? Are we wanted? Are we good enough? We don't ask those questions directly, because we don't have the language. What we do instead is scan. We look at who seems further ahead. Who seems more at ease. Who seems happier, more stable, more successful. We interpret other people's lives as data about our own.

And in some ways, this makes sense. Human beings are social animals. We're wired to use our environment to understand ourselves. From infancy, we develop through imitation. We watch, we absorb, we mirror. Comparison, in that context, isn't pathology—it's development. It helps us learn how to function, how to relate, how to belong.

But at some point, comparison stops being developmental and starts being evaluative. It becomes a way not of learning, but of measuring. And that shift almost always coincides with some kind of emotional uncertainty. When we aren't sure of our value, we look around to see how it's defined. When we aren't sure we're safe, we look to see who is thriving. When we feel unsure of our timing, we study other people's milestones.

And that's where it gets dangerous. Because other people's lives are never neutral. We don't compare ourselves to people we admire gently. We compare ourselves to people who evoke shame. People who trigger that internal narrative that says, "You should be more like them." We zero in on the ones who look polished, confident, accomplished. And we use their image as a mirror, forgetting that it's warped. We never see their full story. Only the surface. And yet we treat that surface like proof.

Comparison, then, becomes a form of emotional self-regulation. We use it to establish direction. But instead of moving us toward ourselves, it pulls us away. It tells us to be faster, thinner, calmer, wealthier, more articulate, more productive. It offers us a checklist of what a "whole" person should look like, and then dares us to try to keep up. And we try. Not because we're shallow or insecure, but because we're looking for something to steady us. Something that says we're okay.

But comparison never actually gives us that. It gives us momentary clarity—a sense of direction or urgency—but it doesn't offer peace. Because it's built on instability. It depends on you seeing yourself as lacking. It depends on you believing that someone else has what you don't. And it never ends. Because no matter how much you grow, there's always someone who seems further along.

It's easy to tell ourselves to stop comparing. But the reality is that most people don't compare out of vanity. They compare because they're scared. Scared of being unremarkable. Scared of wasting time. Scared of being forgotten. Scared of not mattering. And comparison gives shape to that fear. It gives it a name and a face and a target. It tells us that if we could just be more like *them*, everything would settle.

But "them" is a moving target. And more often than not, the people we envy are comparing themselves too. Everyone's chasing an invisible standard that no one fully meets. And in that chase, we lose sight of ourselves—not just our progress, but our desires, our timing, our voice.

There's another reason we lean so heavily on comparison: it offers an illusion of control. When the world feels unpredictable, we want metrics. We want rankings. We want to know where we stand. And comparison gives us that, even if it's artificial. It makes us feel like we're doing something. Like we're assessing the terrain. Like we're making progress. But it's not real progress. It's emotional busywork that keeps us from asking the scarier questions: What do I actually want? What pace feels natural to me? What parts of my life feel borrowed or performative?

Letting go of comparison isn't just about self-esteem. It's about reclaiming orientation from within. It's about finding a new compass that isn't reactive, but rooted. That knows the difference between admiration and self-erasure. That can look at someone else's success and feel inspired—not indicted.

To do that, we have to start noticing the conditions under which comparison spikes. Is it when you're tired? When you're lonely? When something hasn't gone according to plan? Is it when you're scrolling late at night? When you're talking to certain people? When you feel like your life has stalled? These aren't random triggers. They're emotional cues. And comparison is often just the coping strategy that comes next.

Once you identify the pattern, you can start to interrupt it. Not by shaming yourself, but by pausing long enough to ask: What part of me feels unsafe right now? What part of me thinks I'm falling behind? What am I afraid I'm not allowed to want?

Comparison isn't always the enemy. Sometimes it reveals desire. Sometimes it shows us what we value. But we have to be discerning. We have to ask whether the thing we're envying is truly aligned with us—or whether it's just socially rewarded. Whether it reflects a real longing—or whether it's an attempt to soothe an old belief that we're not enough.

Because once we start answering those questions honestly, comparison loses its grip. It stops being a default and becomes a choice. And in that space, we begin to recover something vital: the ability to chart our own path, at our own pace, for reasons that have nothing to do with who's watching.

Visibility and the Social Media Mirror

You don't have to be obsessed with social media to be shaped by it. You don't even have to post. Just being part of a world where visibility is the default alters the way we interpret our own lives. We've moved from a culture of privacy to a culture of performance, and most of us made that transition without even realizing it. We went from living to documenting, from feeling to curating, from becoming to broadcasting. And somewhere in that shift, our understanding of progress, value, and identity got distorted.

Social media doesn't just show us what other people are doing. It shows us how they're being received. We don't just see a promotion—we see the applause. We don't just see a vacation—we see the comments about how much they deserve it. We don't just see a wedding photo—we see a tidal wave of affirmation. The message is clear: being seen is proof of being worthy. Being liked is proof of doing life right.

And so visibility becomes the new currency of legitimacy.

This creates a psychological bind. We begin to believe that our milestones don't count unless they're witnessed. That our joy isn't real unless it gets validated. That our suffering isn't serious unless it's acknowledged publicly. This is not vanity. It's a form of survival in a world where attention is a limited resource. And it deeply impacts the way we experience our own timing.

Before social media, comparison was localized. You measured yourself against people in your school, your workplace, your community. Now, the measuring stick is global. Every scroll exposes you to someone who's younger, more accomplished, more composed, more healed, more successful. And while the rational part of you knows these are curated snapshots, your nervous system doesn't always make that distinction. It sees repetition. And repetition creates emotional truth.

The curated lives we see online function like mirrors, but they're warped. We're not seeing people's full selves. We're seeing the version they've filtered for public consumption. Their best angles. Their most polished insights. Their cleanest recoveries. Their most successful moments. And even when people share their struggles, they're often already in the resolution phase. They're already on the other side, explaining what they learned.

This creates an illusion of coherence. It makes life look linear. Like people just move from insight to growth to triumph in a neat sequence. Like there's a right way to do things, and everyone else has figured it out but you. And when your life doesn't match that rhythm—when your healing is messy, your relationships are complicated, your goals are unclear—it's easy to assume the problem is you.

You begin to question your pace. Your process. Your progress. Not because anything is actually wrong, but because visibility has changed your frame of reference. You no longer measure your life by its felt sense—you measure it by how it compares to what's being publicly celebrated.

The most dangerous part of this isn't the envy. It's the shame. The feeling that you're falling short in a race you didn't even sign up for. The belief that everyone else has cracked the code and you're still fumbling through the basics. The quiet fear that your internal confusion is proof that you're doing life wrong.

This is where visibility becomes a distortion field. It makes us confuse recognition with reality. But recognition is not evenly distributed. Some people are louder, more charismatic, more camera-ready. Some people have more time, more resources, more privilege. Some people have entire teams behind their online presence. And others, like you, might be doing deep, hard, invisible work—without a single post to show for it.

That work still matters. Maybe more than anything that gets posted.

But it can be hard to hold onto that truth when everything around you is optimized for performance. Social media trains us to become brands. To speak in soundbites. To translate our emotional lives into digestible content. And even if we resist that pull, we're still immersed in a digital environment where the metrics of visibility shape how we value ourselves.

You might notice it in subtle ways. The hesitation before sharing something vulnerable. The rush of validation after posting something that resonates. The disappointment when a meaningful moment gets little response. The internal math that starts to develop: what's worth sharing? What sounds impressive? What sounds too needy? Too messy? Too unformed?

This internal negotiation is exhausting. And it can sever us from our actual experiences. We start thinking about how something will look before we fully feel it. We start trying to craft a narrative before we've lived the moment. We start editing ourselves in real time, anticipating how others will perceive us.

It's not wrong to want to be seen. That longing is ancient and human. But the problem with social media is that it offers visibility without intimacy.

We're seen, but not always understood. We're acknowledged, but not always held. And when that becomes our dominant form of connection, we can start to feel lonelier than we did before we ever posted a thing.

The antidote isn't to delete your accounts or swear off scrolling. It's to recalibrate your relationship with visibility. To ask: Who are you when no one is watching? What matters to you when there's no audience? What kinds of growth don't need to be shared in order to be real?

This isn't about withdrawing from the world. It's about remembering that the most meaningful parts of your life often happen off-camera. That progress doesn't have to be posted. That worth doesn't have to be witnessed. That your timeline is valid even if no one applauds it. Especially then.

You're allowed to grow in the dark. You're allowed to be in-process. You're allowed to not know. You're allowed to be building a life that doesn't look remarkable on the outside but feels honest on the inside. That's not failure. That's alignment. That's what real freedom begins to look like.

Your Life vs. The Highlight Reel

You've probably heard the phrase before—"Don't compare your life to someone else's highlight reel." It's meant to be a reminder. A caution against the skewed reality we're exposed to every time we scroll through polished photos, milestone announcements, and clever captions. But the problem with this advice is that it assumes we *can* make that distinction in the moment. That we can keep our critical thinking intact when we're deep in a feed that is designed to make our lives feel incomplete.

Most of us know, intellectually, that social media shows only part of the story. We know people post their wins and crop out their mess. We know the smiling family might be holding it together by a thread. We know the wellness influencer might be battling anxiety behind the camera. And still, when we're vulnerable, tired, doubting ourselves, or longing for something more—our brains absorb those curated images as reality.

What we see begins to reshape what we believe. Not because we're gullible, but because we're human. We absorb patterns. We look for belonging. We want reassurance that we're doing life right. And if everyone else seems to be celebrating, accomplishing, thriving, and posing with soft smiles in well-lit kitchens, it's easy to assume that we're the outlier. That our confusion, our pause, our detours must be a sign of failure.

This illusion becomes even harder to shake because of how linear it looks. Most people don't post during the middle of the process. They post after the resolution. After the promotion comes through. After the relationship is reconciled. After the weight is lost, the baby is born, the trauma is named and claimed and wrapped up in a bow. Even posts about healing are often told from a distance. The struggle is shared, but the present moment is peaceful. The message is clear: transformation should be efficient and public.

But real life doesn't unfold like that. It's not linear. It's layered. You can be healing and still feel broken. You can be succeeding and still feel lost. You can be growing and still feel behind. The highlight reel doesn't make space for these contradictions, so it conditions us to hide them in ourselves. We edit our own lives to appear more coherent. We omit the doubt. We filter the fatigue. We share the lessons, not the rawness. And eventually, we start forgetting what honesty feels like.

Even when we try to be "authentic" online, the framework limits us. The moment you hit post, you're performing, even if unintentionally. You're shaping the story. You're choosing what to show and what to leave out. And while that's not inherently wrong, it does create distance from the full truth of your experience. It turns your life into content. And content, by design, is not meant to be messy. It's meant to be clear, digestible, and engaging.

So what happens when your actual life doesn't feel like content? When it's slow, ordinary, painful, uncertain? What happens when there's nothing to announce, nothing to celebrate, nothing to show? That's when the comparison cuts deepest. Because the highlight reel is always rolling. Someone is always celebrating something. Someone is always hitting a new milestone. And you start to wonder, even in your most grounded moments, whether you're doing something wrong.

That wondering isn't trivial. It shapes how you move. It makes you question your pace, your progress, your process. It makes you want to hurry up and catch up. It makes you feel like you need a breakthrough just to stay relevant. And that urgency is one of the most damaging byproducts of life in comparison culture. It doesn't just make you feel bad—it makes you feel behind. Like your timing is invalid because it doesn't match what's being posted around you.

But here's the truth that never trends: most of life happens off-camera. Most of the growth that matters is slow and quiet. Most of the real breakthroughs don't look like epiphanies. They look like going to bed a little earlier. Speaking up when you usually stay silent. Saying no without explaining yourself. Choosing not to chase something just because it's shiny. Reconnecting with yourself when everything around you tells you to keep performing.

These moments don't get likes. But they change your life.

What would it look like to stop chasing the highlight reel? To stop organizing your story around what will look good or sound impressive? To start trusting that your pace, your path, your rhythm is enough—even when it doesn't feel like progress?

It would look like freedom. Not the loud kind, but the quiet kind. The kind that lets you delete an app and feel more connected, not less. The kind that lets you celebrate privately without needing an audience. The kind that lets you make meaning for yourself instead of waiting for someone else to validate it.

Your life doesn't have to follow a narrative arc. It doesn't need to be "post-worthy" to be worth living. It doesn't have to resemble anyone else's timeline, caption, or curated aesthetic. You're allowed to be in the middle of something messy. You're allowed to not know what comes next. You're allowed to build a life that doesn't perform well, but feels real.

And when you forget that—which you will, because we all do—come back to this question: Would I still be doing what I'm doing if no one could see it? If the answer is yes, that's where your truth lives. That's where your life begins again. Not in the highlight reel, but in the quiet, beautiful honesty of your own unfolding.

* * *

3

Burnout Disguised as Self-Doubt

There comes a point—quiet but unmistakable—when your body starts to slow down before your mind agrees to it. Tasks that used to feel simple now feel heavy. Concentration slips. Your motivation disappears without warning. You find yourself rereading the same sentence, forgetting the thing you walked into the room to do, skipping the small rituals that once gave your day shape. You're tired, but not in a way that sleep can fix. And when you try to explain it, you hear yourself say things like I'm just not trying hard enough or I can't seem to get it together.

What you don't say—but what lingers underneath—is this: I think something might be wrong with me.

That feeling, that quiet spiral of internal blame, is what makes burnout so difficult to spot. Because it doesn't always announce itself as physical collapse. It often shows up as shame. You don't just feel depleted. You feel behind. Embarrassed. Guilty. You assume you're unmotivated, disorganized, falling short. You look around and think, Other people seem to be managing this—why can't I?

Burnout in this form is difficult to name because we've been trained to treat exhaustion like a character flaw. We don't ask what systems are draining us. We ask why we can't keep up. And instead of resting, we double down. We push harder. We search for discipline, for hacks, for the next productivity method. But beneath all of that effort is one quietly devastating belief: If I were stronger, this wouldn't be happening.

That belief is the lie burnout tells. And it's one we need to examine with care, because the stakes are high. When exhaustion is mistaken for inadequacy, we don't get help. We don't slow down. We don't recalibrate. We just criticize ourselves into deeper depletion. And by the time we finally stop, we're not just tired—we're disconnected from ourselves entirely.

In this chapter, we'll take a deeper look at how burnout morphs into self-doubt, how our culture actively rewards the appearance of thriving while ignoring the cost, how survival mode gets mislabeled as laziness, and what it means to reframe your exhaustion not as failure, but as a valid signal from a system that was never designed to support your full humanity.

Because you don't lack motivation. You lack margins. You don't need more discipline. You need restoration. And you're not falling short. You're carrying more than anyone knows.

The Collapse Point

It doesn't always happen all at once. Sometimes the collapse arrives gradually. A dropped obligation here. A forgotten appointment there. A text you mean to respond to but can't find the words. Other times, it's immediate—a deadline missed, a breakdown in the middle of a workday, an emotional outburst you didn't see coming. However it happens, the moment is unmistakable. Your functioning drops below your usual threshold, and everything in you begins to panic. Not because of what you've done, but because of what it means. You start asking yourself the scariest question of all: What if I can't pull it together?

This is the collapse point. And most people don't recognize it for what it is. Instead of identifying it as burnout, they treat it as failure. Instead of seeing it as a full-body signal, they translate it as a moral indictment. I'm falling apart. I'm behind. I'm not who I used to be. That last one is especially common. Because the collapse point doesn't just disrupt your routines—it disrupts your self-concept. The part of you that's always managed, always pushed through, always taken pride in being capable—that part suddenly doesn't show up.

And when you've built your worth on functioning, losing that capacity feels like losing yourself.

But let's be clear: collapse is not the result of weakness. It's the inevitable outcome of chronic emotional overextension. When your nervous system has been running on adrenaline and coping for too long without rest, without acknowledgment, without repair, it doesn't just get tired—it gets protective. It begins to shut down what's nonessential. Focus. Motivation. Language. Emotional tolerance. You don't choose it. Your body chooses it for you. Because it's trying to preserve you.

The tragedy is that our culture doesn't recognize this kind of collapse as legitimate. Unless there's a physical illness or a visible crisis, we assume people are fine. We assume they're just unmotivated. We assume they've become unreliable. Even within ourselves, we hold that same standard. You're not bleeding. You're not in the hospital. You're still showing up. So what's the problem?

The problem is that functioning can become its own disguise. You can be performing at work, responding to emails, making meals, and still be internally collapsing. You can be smiling in meetings while your mind is foggy, your body is tense, your emotions are muted. But because you're still "doing," you don't feel like you have the right to say you're struggling.

That's the lie of performance culture. It tells us that if you can still produce, then you're fine. But burnout doesn't wait until you stop producing. It starts long before that—when the quality of your presence disappears. When you go through the motions but feel disconnected from yourself. When you look at your calendar and feel dread instead of purpose. When everything begins to feel like too much, but you can't name why.

The collapse point is not a failure of willpower. It's a failure of design. Most people are not meant to sustain the emotional load they're carrying—especially those who are managing invisible labor. Caregiving. Identity stress. Racial fatigue. Hypervigilance in unsafe environments. Trauma processing in silence. These burdens don't show up in to-do lists, but they erode the nervous system all the same. And when there's no space to process, no pause to recalibrate, the system eventually defaults to protection mode.

Unfortunately, protection doesn't always look helpful. It can look like procrastination. Irritability. Withdrawal. Shutdown. It can look like a loss of motivation, a drop in communication, a dip in creativity. And without the right framework, we misinterpret those symptoms. We call them laziness. Flakiness. Flaws. We punish ourselves for what is actually a deeply intelligent response to sustained overload.

What's worse is that many of us have been praised for ignoring our early signals. We were told we were strong when we pushed through. We were told we were reliable when we suppressed our needs. We were told we were resilient when we kept showing up despite the cost. And so we internalized the belief that collapse is something to be ashamed of. That rest is indulgent. That burnout is personal failure.

It's not. It's the body and mind finally refusing to betray themselves any longer.

But by the time the collapse comes, self-blame has usually already arrived. You might start saying things like I'm so behind or I can't believe I let it get this bad or Everyone else seems to be managing. You might try to compensate—by over-apologizing, by making promises you can't keep, by forcing yourself back into routines before you're ready. You try to convince yourself that if you can just get back on track, the shame will go away.

But the real healing doesn't happen through force. It happens through recognition. You have to see the collapse for what it is: a boundary your body set when you couldn't. A protest your system made on your behalf. A moment of reckoning, not because you failed, but because you've been carrying too much, too quietly, for too long.

And that shift—from self-blame to self-understanding—isn't just semantic. It's physiological. When you stop interpreting your fatigue as a flaw, your nervous system begins to settle. Your mind stops attacking itself. You stop leaking energy into shame, and you begin redirecting it toward repair. You begin asking different questions—not How do I fix this? but What has this been trying to tell me?

That's where the healing begins.

Because collapse is not the end of your story. It's a turning point. A moment of clarity. A chance to stop pretending you're fine when you're not. A chance to rewrite your relationship to productivity, to value, to self-respect. And most of all, a chance to begin again—not from the version of you that's burned out and scrambling, but from the part of you that's finally ready to live in alignment with your actual limits, your actual needs, and your actual truth.

Capitalism and the Invisibility of Fatigue

We live in a culture that treats exhaustion as a badge of honor. Being tired is no longer seen as a warning sign—it's seen as a normal state of existence, even a respectable one. When someone says they're swamped or slammed or "barely hanging in," we nod with recognition, sometimes even admiration. We reward busyness. We glorify overwork. We celebrate hustle. And in the background of all of that is a system that runs on one very profitable myth: that your worth is tied to your output.

This is not a personal mindset. It's an economic structure. Capitalism doesn't just sell goods and services. It sells identity. It tells us that value is earned through production, and rest is justified only if it increases future productivity. It infiltrates not just our jobs, but our inner lives. Our hobbies become side hustles. Our healing becomes optimized. Our routines become performance. Even leisure becomes something to curate and document—proof that we're still using our time wisely.

And when that framework becomes internalized, fatigue no longer feels like a signal. It feels like failure.

It's not just that we're tired. It's that we're not allowed to show it. We push through the day with a practiced smile, answer emails with urgency even when we're depleted, and apologize when we need to take a break—as if tending to our limits requires permission. There's a reason for this: in capitalist culture, fatigue is invisible on purpose. The system doesn't want us to stop and feel what's happening. It wants us to keep producing. And if we can't do that joyfully, then at least we can do it quietly.

Work culture reinforces this invisibility at every turn. Companies talk about self-care while expecting after-hours availability. Job postings demand flexibility but offer little support. Colleagues praise each other for "powering through," while silently competing over who's more overwhelmed. And even in professions that should be rooted in care—education, health, mental health, service—workers are pushed to the brink with the unspoken message that fatigue is just part of the job.

This doesn't just impact our performance. It distorts our self-perception. When you live in a system that only values visible results, it's easy to assume that your exhaustion is a personal problem. You forget that you're running on limited sleep, managing invisible labor, absorbing constant digital input, navigating personal grief, and being bombarded by cultural trauma. You forget that the game is rigged. And instead, you turn the pressure inward: I should be able to handle this.

But the truth is, most people are handling far more than anyone can see. Especially those who live in marginalized bodies. For many, fatigue isn't just physical—it's emotional. It's the cost of constant code-switching. Of enduring microaggressions without reacting. Of always being the one to explain or represent. Of doing the same job as others with less pay, fewer resources, and more scrutiny. These layers of fatigue rarely get named in professional settings. They're invisible by design. And yet they erode the nervous system just as fast—if not faster.

Invisibility also shows up in the emotional realm. You might be exhausted from pretending you're okay. From keeping it together for your family. From being the strong one. From masking your anxiety. From surviving while also trying to grow. But because your exhaustion doesn't have a diagnosis or a visible crisis, it doesn't feel valid. You minimize it. You tell yourself other people have it worse. You feel guilty for wanting to rest.

And the system counts on that. It counts on your silence. On your self-blame. On your willingness to keep going even when your body says stop. That's what makes burnout so hard to interrupt. The moment you begin to slow down, the internal voice of capitalism starts to whisper: You're falling behind. You'll lose momentum. You're being selfish. You'll become irrelevant.

That voice is not your intuition. It's your training.

To unlearn that voice, you have to name it. You have to see how deeply the system has embedded itself into your self-worth. You have to recognize that rest is not a reward—it's a requirement. That productivity is not the same as purpose. That you are not lazy just because you are no longer willing to sacrifice your well-being for the appearance of competence.

And this isn't just about individual recovery. It's about collective reclamation. Because the more we normalize the visibility of fatigue, the harder it becomes for systems to ignore it. When people begin to name their limits, advocate for humane workloads, reject performative self-care, and prioritize sustainability over optics, the culture begins to shift. Slowly, but powerfully.

Of course, not everyone has the same access to rest. Not everyone can take breaks without consequences. That's why individual self-care can never be the full solution. We need systemic change. We need work environments that honor human rhythms. We need communities that recognize invisible labor. We need policies that support recovery, not just resilience.

But even within those limitations, there is room to begin. You can start by noticing how fatigue shows up in your life—not just physically, but emotionally and cognitively. You can start by interrupting the instinct to apologize for your needs. You can start by asking: What if I didn't have to prove I'm tired in order to be allowed to rest?

Because that's the heart of it. Capitalism trains us to believe we must earn everything—including our recovery. But you don't need to collapse in order to be deserving. You don't need to explain every detail in order to justify a pause. Your fatigue is real. Your limits are sacred. And your right to rest was never supposed to depend on how visible your suffering is.

Survival Mode and the False Story of Laziness

If you've ever called yourself lazy, there's a good chance you weren't. Not really. You were probably overwhelmed. Stuck. Disconnected. Exhausted. But because we don't have many culturally accepted words for those states—especially when they show up without a dramatic backstory—we default to the one that stings the most and explains the least: lazy.

Laziness, as we use the word today, isn't really a description of behavior.

It's a moral accusation. It implies a failure of will, a defect in character. And yet, when you look closely at the people who carry that label—whether from others or from themselves—they're almost always burdened. Not indifferent. Not careless. Not unmotivated. Just buried beneath too much: too many expectations, too many unresolved emotions, too many unacknowledged fears, and not nearly enough support.

What we often call laziness is actually a nervous system stuck in survival mode.

Survival mode is what happens when the body prioritizes safety over everything else. When you're under threat—physical, emotional, psychological—your system reroutes its energy. Blood flow changes. Focus narrows. Decision-making stalls. Complex tasks become nearly impossible, not because you're weak, but because your brain has shifted into triage. It's trying to conserve energy, simplify demands, and stay ready for whatever might come next.

This is not a conscious process. You don't choose to shut down. You don't choose to freeze in front of the simplest task. You don't choose to scroll endlessly or delay important decisions or leave things half-finished. These are not strategic choices. They are symptoms of a system trying to protect itself.

But when those symptoms show up—especially in environments that prize productivity over wellness—they're judged harshly. You're seen as unreliable. Unmotivated. Disengaged. You start hearing it from others, or you start telling it to yourself. And because the shame of being "lazy" is so powerful, you try to push through. You try to override your body. You try to power up, focus harder, get your act together.

Sometimes it works—briefly. You meet the deadline. You reply to the email. You drag yourself through the motions. But the cost is steep. Because every time you override your internal signals in service of performance, you reinforce the belief that your body can't be trusted, that your needs are weaknesses, and that your energy only matters when it results in output.

Eventually, even pushing doesn't work. Your nervous system stops responding to urgency. Your executive function breaks down. You forget things you've always remembered. You can't organize your thoughts. Your emotions feel muted or volatile. And once again, the word lazy rises to the surface. But by this point, it's not just inaccurate—it's cruel.

What's actually happening is collapse. Not dramatic, all-at-once collapse, but slow, cumulative erosion. The kind that comes from long-term stress, from unresolved grief, from emotional labor that's been invisible for years. And in that state, everything feels hard. Making decisions. Initiating tasks. Following through. Even resting doesn't feel restorative, because the guilt doesn't let you fully release.

This is where executive dysfunction kicks in. A term more often associated with ADHD or other neurodivergent conditions, but just as applicable to anyone whose nervous system has been overwhelmed. Executive dysfunction isn't a mindset problem. It's a cognitive disruption. It makes it hard to plan, prioritize, and start—even things you care about. And it gets worse under pressure, shame, and self-criticism.

So what do most people do? They call it laziness. They internalize the struggle as proof of their inadequacy. And the cycle repeats.

But what if we called it what it really is? What if, instead of asking "Why am I so lazy?" we asked "What part of me is overburdened?" or "What am I afraid will happen if I slow down?" or "What internal threat is my system reacting to right now?"

These questions don't offer quick fixes. But they shift the frame. They replace judgment with inquiry. They open the door to compassion. And compassion, more than motivation or willpower, is what helps people move forward.

Because survival mode doesn't end through shame. It ends through safety.

You start to exit survival mode when your system begins to trust that it won't be punished for resting. When it senses that slowness is allowed. When it realizes that value doesn't have to be earned through suffering. When it's no longer being asked to perform while starving for repair.

And exiting survival mode doesn't always look productive. At first, it might look like doing less. Like letting go of perfection. Like not replying right away. Like resting even when your to-do list isn't done. These acts might feel wrong at first—lazy, even. But they're not. They're reorienting. They're the nervous system starting to recalibrate after years of pushing past its limits.

Eventually, something shifts. You notice that your energy comes back in small waves. That tasks you avoided no longer feel threatening. That your thoughts are clearer, your mood more stable, your capacity returning. Not because you forced yourself out of your slump, but because you stopped treating your depletion like a flaw.

You can't shame yourself into functioning. You can't bully your system into clarity. What you can do is listen. Listen to what your mind is afraid of. Listen to what your body is asking for. Listen to the stories you inherited about laziness and rest and earning your place. And then choose—carefully, consciously—not to repeat them.

Laziness is not the story. It's the misinterpretation. The real story is capacity. And capacity, like anything else human, fluctuates. It contracts. It expands. It needs tending. And most of all, it needs respect.

You are not broken because you're tired. You are not defective because your system has limits. And you are not lazy because you can't meet a standard that was never built with your full humanity in mind.

Reframing the Burnout Spiral

Burnout is not a singular event. It's not something that happens once, is "fixed," and then disappears. It's a cycle. A spiral. A pattern of overextension and collapse, pressure and paralysis, hyper-functioning and deep shame. And unless we understand what keeps that cycle in motion, we can spend years treating the symptoms without ever addressing the engine underneath.

The burnout spiral begins quietly. It often starts with overcommitment—saying yes too often, trying to prove something, trying to stay ahead, trying not to fall behind. It might come from ambition, or from anxiety. Sometimes both. You push yourself to meet expectations, internal and external. You tell yourself it's just a busy season. That you'll rest soon. That it's fine.

And then, the symptoms begin to creep in. You feel tired but wired. You lose small details. Your sleep changes. Your emotions get flatter or more reactive. You start to dread things that once felt manageable. You try to push through, and for a while, you might succeed. But the cost compounds. And eventually, your system hits a wall.

This is where the shame shows up. You stop being able to function at your normal level, and instead of interpreting this as a sign of burnout, you interpret it as a personal failure. You tell yourself you've let people down. You feel guilty for slowing down. You start to question your identity. And all of that shame doesn't create relief—it creates pressure. Pressure to get back to normal. Pressure to prove you're okay. Pressure to stop "making excuses" and get your act together.

So you push again. You override your exhaustion. You do what needs to be done. And because you're capable, it works—for a little while. But you never fully recover. You just suppress. And the next time burnout creeps in, it hits harder. Your window for resilience gets smaller. Your energy disappears faster. Your sense of self becomes more fragile. And the spiral continues.

Most people don't recognize how deep this pattern runs until it's disrupted. Maybe they crash. Maybe they quit. Maybe their body forces them to stop. And when that happens, they're often left with a terrifying realization: I don't know how to rest without guilt. I don't know who I am without the doing. I don't know how to be with myself when I'm not performing.

This is not because they're weak. It's because they've been trained to equate worth with effort. Trained to believe that rest must be earned. Trained to view exhaustion not as information, but as evidence of deficiency.

But here's the truth: burnout doesn't mean you're not trying hard enough. It often means you've been trying for too long without enough support. Without enough recovery. Without enough permission to be a full person, not just a productive one.

To interrupt the burnout spiral, we have to start asking different questions. Not "How do I get back to normal?" but "What was I calling normal that led me here in the first place?" Not "How do I become more disciplined?" but "What parts of me are trying to be heard through this exhaustion?" Not "What's wrong with me?" but "What has my body been trying to tell me that I haven't yet listened to?"

These questions reframe burnout from a character flaw to a communication pattern. They remind us that our systems are always speaking, even when we've stopped listening.

Because burnout is not just about work. It's about relational depletion. It's about emotional suppression. It's about caretaking without reciprocity, performing without rest, showing up without being seen. It's about saying yes when we mean maybe, staying silent when we need to speak, minimizing our needs because we don't want to be a burden.

And most of all, burnout is about disconnection. From our rhythms. From our intuition. From our right to pause.

Reframing the burnout spiral means learning to recognize the early signs—not just in your schedule, but in your spirit. It means noticing when your creativity disappears, when your body feels heavy, when your thoughts get noisy, when you're over-apologizing, when your joy feels like a memory instead of a possibility.

It means slowing down *before* you collapse. It means redefining what success looks like. It means building lives that honor the reality of being human instead of pretending we're machines.

And yes, that kind of shift is uncomfortable. It forces you to unlearn everything you were praised for: your efficiency, your self-sacrifice, your ability to push through. It asks you to start trusting feelings you used to suppress. To start honoring needs you used to ignore. To start believing that you are still worthy even when you're not performing.

That's not easy. But it's necessary. Because the cost of staying in the spiral isn't just fatigue—it's the gradual erosion of your internal world. The disconnection from your own values. The shrinking of your aliveness. And you deserve more than that. You deserve a life that feels sustainable. A life that includes rest, not just recovery. Slowness, not just stillness. Integrity, not just output.

There is no productivity hack that will heal burnout. What will heal it is a complete reorientation toward your own limits, your own rhythms, your own right to exist without constant justification.

Burnout is not the end of your story. It's a signal. And if you learn to listen, it will take you not just back to yourself—but forward into a life you no longer have to recover from.

* * *

4

The Optimization Trap

You don't have to be obsessed with self-help to feel like there's always something to improve. Even the most grounded among us have likely, at some point, thought: I need to be more productive. I need to fix my mindset. I need to get more efficient, more balanced, more emotionally resilient. And while there's nothing inherently wrong with growth, there's a sharp edge to the way we're being told to pursue it. Somewhere along the way, personal development stopped being a journey and became an expectation.

We live in a culture where optimization is no longer just a goal—it's a default setting. There's always a new method to try, a better habit to build, a mindset to refine. Your morning routine can be hacked. Your nervous system can be trained. Your relationships can be upgraded. Your sleep tracked, your attention sharpened, your gut biome tested and adjusted. Nothing is off-limits. Nothing is ever quite enough.

At first, it feels empowering. The promise of self-improvement offers hope. It makes change feel possible. But for many people, it becomes a cycle of quiet desperation. You're always chasing the next breakthrough. The next upgrade. The next version of yourself that will finally feel right. And in the process, you stop asking a more fundamental question: Why do I believe I need to be fixed in the first place?

This chapter is about that question.

It's about the emotional undercurrent beneath the optimization culture.

The hunger it feeds. The shame it quietly reinforces. The way it capitalizes on the belief that rest is only allowed once you've earned it. That healing is only valid if it produces results. That who you are right now is only a draft of who you're supposed to become.

We'll explore why the self-improvement industry is so seductive, how self-discipline can quietly mutate into self-punishment, why the myth of potential is often rooted in early emotional wounds, and what it actually means to live as though you're already enough—even when the world insists otherwise.

Because the truth is, you are not a project. You are a person. And no amount of optimization will make you more human. Only more exhausted.

Always One Fix Away

There's a strange kind of comfort in believing that the next fix will finally make things better. A new routine, a better habit, the right podcast, the right program, the right planner. A tweak here, a breakthrough there. It's not quite desperation—but it's close. It's an emotional hunger dressed up as ambition. And in a culture obsessed with self-improvement, it becomes easy to mistake that hunger for hope.

This is the promise at the heart of the optimization trap: that you are only one fix away from being your best self. It's an attractive idea. Clean. Actionable. Empowering, even. It says you're not stuck—you just haven't figured it out yet. There's always another system, another method, another insight that will make everything click. You're just one step away from being fully functional, emotionally grounded, wildly productive, and finally—finally—at peace.

But here's the deeper truth: most people chasing that fix are not doing so from a place of empowerment. They're doing it from a place of inadequacy.

And that's what makes the self-help and biohacking industries so profitable. They don't sell healing. They sell relief from self-disgust. From shame. From the anxiety of never feeling like you're quite there. They present tools and strategies as solutions to a problem you were trained to believe about yourself: that who you are, as you are, is not enough.

This doesn't mean that self-help is inherently harmful. Many tools and ideas are valuable. Some practices truly do support growth. But it's not just the tool that matters—it's the *emotional logic* behind using it. Are you trying to support your well-being, or are you trying to earn your right to exist?

That difference is everything.

Because if your motivation is shame-based—if it's rooted in the belief that you're fundamentally falling short—then no fix will ever feel like enough. You'll implement the routine, then raise the bar. You'll finish the course, then find another. You'll meet the goal, then feel guilty for not aiming higher. The target keeps moving, not because the tools don't work, but because the part of you using them doesn't believe it deserves to rest.

I've seen this pattern in students, professionals, spiritual seekers, trauma survivors, and everyday people trying to hold it together. They're not shallow. They're not superficial. They're trying. Desperately. They're devouring books, listening to every expert, customizing their supplements and scheduling their gratitude practice—and still feeling behind.

That feeling doesn't come from failure. It comes from a belief that healing, success, or peace is something to *achieve*, rather than something to *inhabit*.

And that belief is often old. It starts young. The child who learns that love is earned tries harder. The teenager who isn't allowed to rest becomes hyper-productive. The adult who internalizes perfection as protection becomes a master of self-regulation—but forgets how to feel safe.

And so when optimization culture enters the scene, it doesn't feel manipulative. It feels familiar. It offers a framework for self-worth. It says: you're not broken—you're just unoptimized. And if you follow these five steps, you can finally become the version of yourself that deserves ease.

The cruelty of this promise is not just that it's false. It's that it sounds so reasonable. It's hard to argue with wanting to improve. And most of us don't. We want to grow. We want to understand ourselves. We want to function better. But growth and healing are not the same as constant fixing. And functioning is not the same as flourishing.

Real growth includes discomfort. Uncertainty. Backward steps. Days where you forget everything you've learned. Real healing doesn't follow a checklist. It's cyclical, relational, sometimes messy. But optimization culture doesn't leave room for that. It demands progress that can be tracked, milestones that can be measured, and results that can be shared.

That's why it feels like a trap. Because even when you're doing everything right, you still feel like you're failing.

So how do you know when you're caught in this pattern? The signs are subtle. You might feel like you're always preparing to live better, but never actually living. You might feel like your worth is tied to your next breakthrough. You might feel like rest is a waste of time unless it makes you more productive. You might feel like you're chasing clarity but becoming more anxious. You might even find that your search for self-improvement is getting in the way of actual self-connection.

And if that's true, the answer is not to try harder. The answer is to pause and ask: what am I trying to fix that might not actually be broken?

Because the truth is, you're not one fix away from becoming whole. You already are. You may be wounded. You may be tired. You may be carrying more than your share. But you are not unfinished. You are not a constant repair project. You are not someone who only deserves gentleness once you've earned it.

What if the next chapter of your growth isn't about improving yourself—but about believing that you don't need to be improved in order to be valid?

What if all the fixing is a distraction from what actually needs attention—the part of you that's afraid to be still?

That's where the work begins. Not in finding the next fix, but in learning to stay with yourself when nothing feels resolved. In realizing that your value is not in your progress, but in your presence.

When Self-Discipline Becomes Self-Punishment

Discipline is one of those words we're taught to admire from a young age. It's framed as the key to success, to self-respect, to emotional maturity. It's what separates the "serious" from the unserious, the accomplished from the mediocre, the healthy from the indulgent. If you're disciplined, you're winning at life. If you're not, you're letting yourself down.

But for many people, what gets labeled as discipline is something else entirely. It's not self-respect. It's not structure. It's not growth. It's control. Fear-based control, shame-based control, trauma-based control. And over time, that kind of control doesn't build self-trust. It erodes it. It turns every unmet expectation into a referendum on your character. Every skipped workout, every missed meditation, every day off-plan becomes evidence that you're failing, slacking, backsliding. And you punish yourself accordingly—with tighter rules, harsher language, smaller margins for error.

This is where discipline becomes self-punishment. And it often happens so quietly that we don't notice the shift. One day you're building a new habit because it feels good. You're getting up early, journaling, eating clean, tracking progress. But somewhere along the way, the "why" gets lost. The goal becomes about maintenance, perfection, consistency at all costs. And if you deviate—even for good reason—you feel like you've betrayed yourself.

That feeling isn't about the behavior. It's about the internalized belief that your worth is conditional on your performance.

This is especially common among high achievers, trauma survivors, people raised in rigid or emotionally inconsistent homes, and those who found early safety in control. For them, discipline wasn't just a tool—it was a shield. A way to manage chaos, to stay one step ahead of judgment, to make themselves acceptable in systems that didn't offer unconditional belonging.

And because it worked—at least for a while—they assumed it was the only way.

But control is not the same as safety. And discipline is not the same as care.

You can wake up at 5 a.m. every day and still hate yourself. You can meet all your goals and still feel hollow. You can be externally organized and internally anxious, driven by fear that any deviation will unravel the whole thing.

That's not structure. That's survival.

And the survival version of discipline is exhausting. Because it's rooted in fear of collapse. If I rest, I won't start again. If I stop tracking, I'll lose control. If I slow down, I'll disappear. These thoughts don't come from laziness or weakness. They come from pain. From a nervous system that has equated stillness with danger. From a belief that you're only safe when you're producing, improving, pushing forward.

So what starts as a wellness routine can easily become a cycle of self-surveillance. You're always watching yourself. Policing your urges. Measuring your progress. You start to speak to yourself like a drill sergeant. You lose compassion for your own fluctuations. You treat imperfection like a moral failure.

And worst of all, it can look like success.

That's what makes it so hard to challenge. Because you're meeting deadlines. You're getting compliments. You're admired for your willpower. People ask you how you stay so consistent. But no one sees the panic that sets in when you consider skipping a workout. No one sees the shame spiral when you deviate from your plan. No one sees how fragile it all feels beneath the surface.

This kind of discipline doesn't build resilience. It builds fragility dressed up as control. Because when your structure is rooted in fear, it can't tolerate disruption. It can't adapt. It can't rest. And eventually, it breaks.

So what does real discipline look like? The kind that's rooted in care, not control?

It looks like flexibility. It looks like knowing when to push and when to pause. It looks like respecting your energy levels instead of overriding them. It looks like returning to your routines without shame after you've stepped away. It looks like holding goals lightly, not like weapons. It looks like being able to say: I matter even when I don't perform.

That kind of discipline is sustainable. Because it doesn't rely on fear. It relies on trust. Trust that your worth isn't up for debate. Trust that your value doesn't disappear when your routines fall apart. Trust that you can grow without punishing yourself into submission.

But building that kind of trust requires a reckoning. You have to unlearn the idea that control is virtue. That exhaustion is evidence of commitment. That deprivation is discipline. You have to start asking: Who taught me that I needed to be this hard on myself? What am I afraid will happen if I loosen the grip?

And you have to grieve the part of you that believed punishment was the only path to progress.

This grief is real. Because for many people, control was safety. Discipline was love. Rigidity was the only thing that kept them afloat. Letting go can feel terrifying. But on the other side of that fear is something gentler, more enduring—a self-respect that doesn't rely on performance, a self-trust that doesn't collapse under imperfection, a discipline that includes rest, softness, and the right to evolve.

You don't have to earn your way into wholeness. You don't have to push yourself to the edge to be valid. And you don't have to treat your body, your mind, or your spirit like a machine in need of optimization.

Real growth is spacious. Real change is patient. And real discipline is never a form of punishment—it's a form of love.

The Myth of "Reaching Potential"

There's a phrase that floats through our lives like a permanent measuring stick: reaching your potential. It sounds noble. Aspirational. The kind of thing we're supposed to strive for. You have so much potential. You're capable of more. Don't waste your gifts. From childhood, many of us are praised for our promise, pushed to fulfill it, haunted by the idea that there's a better, more fully realized version of ourselves just out of reach—and it's our job to get there.

But what's rarely questioned is the emotional cost of that phrase. Because for a lot of people, the concept of potential doesn't feel like encouragement. It feels like pressure. A quiet, lifelong pressure to constantly become, improve, refine, excel. And under that pressure is a dangerous assumption: that who you are right now is not quite it. That your current self is just a draft. And until you reach some invisible standard, you are unfinished.

This is how the myth of potential becomes a trap.

It takes a natural human desire for growth and turns it into a kind of emotional debt. It frames your life as a race toward an idealized version of yourself, and anything less than that becomes a kind of failure. You start treating your present state as something to fix, rather than something to inhabit. And even when you make progress, it rarely feels like enough. Because the target keeps moving. And the self you're trying to become always feels just a little out of reach.

This myth is especially powerful for people who were labeled as "gifted," "talented," "mature for their age," or "old souls." The praise comes early, and it comes with a subtext: you are valuable because of your potential. Not because of your presence. Not because of your joy. Not because of your aliveness. Because of what you might become. Because of how well you can perform.

That's not love. That's performance-based affection.

And it leaves a mark. Adults who were raised on that kind of praise often carry an invisible weight. They're high functioning, often successful, but chronically dissatisfied. They keep raising the bar. They accomplish things that others admire—but rarely stop to feel the accomplishment. Because the voice inside says: you're still not there. You could be doing more.

For many, this internal pressure becomes part of their identity. They don't know who they are without a project. Without a mountain to climb. Without some better version of themselves waiting to be reached. Stillness becomes intolerable. Rest feels like regression. And slowness, softness, or uncertainty gets interpreted as personal failure.

What's missing from the conversation about potential is context. No one talks about the emotional labor of trying to constantly improve. No one talks about how trauma, chronic stress, or systemic oppression affects someone's capacity to "fulfill their potential." No one asks whether the pursuit of potential is even coming from the self—or whether it was internalized from someone else's dream, someone else's pressure, someone else's unhealed story.

And no one says this: maybe potential isn't something to chase. Maybe it's something to release.

Because the very idea of potential is built on a binary—you either reach it or you don't. You either become what you're supposed to be, or you fall short. But human lives aren't that simple. They're complex, messy, nonlinear. They're full of detours, regressions, late starts, redefinitions. And often, the moments that matter most don't look like milestones. They look like pauses.

Breakdowns. New beginnings that don't make sense on a timeline.

When you start looking at life through a trauma-informed lens, the myth of potential begins to unravel. You start to see that many people's so-called underperformance is actually self-protection. That what looks like procrastination or wasted talent is often the result of unprocessed pain. That what gets interpreted as laziness or avoidance might actually be someone trying to heal.

You also start to realize that the pressure to maximize yourself is not neutral. It's often a reflection of capitalism, perfectionism, or family systems that equate worth with output. And when that pressure gets embedded early, it becomes a part of your nervous system. You feel it in the quiet moments. The sense that you should be doing more, knowing more, becoming more.

And when you're not, you feel defective. Like you're failing at life. Like you've let yourself down.

But what if you haven't failed? What if you've been surviving? What if the time you think you've lost wasn't wasted—but was necessary for healing, grounding, learning to live without self-abandonment?

What if the version of you that's not chasing anything is still worthy?

Reframing the idea of potential doesn't mean giving up on growth. It means refusing to let your life be defined by a moving target. It means learning to see growth not as a vertical climb, but as a widening—a deepening into self-trust, self-knowledge, and self-respect. It means recognizing that some of the most important shifts in life can't be measured in goals or milestones. They're felt in the body, in relationships, in the moments where you finally stop performing and start simply being.

And most importantly, it means letting go of the belief that your current self is just a placeholder for a better one.

You are not a prototype. You are a person. You are allowed to grow slowly. You are allowed to change your mind. You are allowed to do less, to want less, to be less efficient. You are allowed to be joyful without being productive. You are allowed to be still.

There is no prize for reaching your potential. There is only the present moment—and your ability to meet it with honesty, softness, and the courage to believe that maybe you are already enough.

Enough Without Earning It

Somewhere along the way, we learned that being enough was a status you had to earn. Not a birthright. Not a baseline. But something conditional—awarded based on how well you perform, how little you complain, how much you give, and how much you achieve. You don't just get to be enough. You have to deserve it.

And if you're not actively deserving it—if you're tired, if you're messy, if you're behind, if you're unsure—then the sense of enoughness starts to fade. It feels like something you lost, or worse, like something you never had.

This belief doesn't come out of nowhere. It's often shaped in early childhood, in homes where affection was tied to behavior, where achievement got more attention than presence, where love was stable but conditional. Maybe you were the responsible one. The star. The fixer. Maybe you were praised for being helpful, being strong, being independent. Maybe your needs were inconvenient. Maybe you learned that to be loved, you had to be impressive.

So you kept proving yourself. Over and over. In school, in work, in relationships. You performed competence. You apologized for rest. You mistook approval for belonging. You told yourself: if I can just do more, give more, be more, I'll finally feel like I'm enough.

But that finish line never arrives. Because it doesn't exist.

What no one tells you is that the habit of self-negotiation—this idea that you have to earn your place in the world—becomes so ingrained that even when the pressure isn't external, it keeps showing up internally. It becomes the background noise of your daily life. You can't relax. You can't stop planning. You can't sit still in your own worth without looking for evidence that you've earned it.

You might even take pride in how hard you work to be enough. In your high standards. Your discipline. Your refusal to settle. But deep down, that pride is often covering fear. Fear that if you stop trying, everything will fall apart. That if you don't keep proving yourself, people will see through you. That if you don't keep up the effort, you'll become invisible, or worse—disappointing.

And yet, in moments of clarity—usually when you're exhausted, cracked open, raw—something else whispers through: I am so tired of trying to earn my own humanity.

Because that's what's really at stake here. Not just performance. Not just success. But the core belief about whether your existence is inherently valid. Whether you are allowed to take up space without justification. Whether you are allowed to need rest, to fall apart, to be incomplete and still be seen as whole.

That's what the myth of earned enoughness steals from us: the right to be human.

We see this myth reinforced everywhere. In workplaces that reward burnout. In relationships that measure worth by how little someone asks for. In self-help language that frames healing as a checklist. In systems that only grant dignity to those who contribute. Even in our own language: "I'm not doing enough. I haven't earned a break. I don't feel like I deserve this."

Deserve. As if goodness has to be proven.

But what if it didn't?

What if enoughness wasn't something to attain—but something to return to?

That doesn't mean giving up on growth. It doesn't mean settling or avoiding responsibility. It means starting from a different foundation. A place where growth is driven by curiosity, not shame. Where effort is a choice, not a debt. Where rest is seen as wisdom, not weakness. Where your value isn't up for constant reassessment.

It means beginning to ask a different set of questions.

Instead of: Am I doing enough?

Try: What would change if I already believed I was?

Instead of: How do I earn my worth?

Try: What if it was never in question?

Instead of: What's wrong with me?

Try: What am I carrying that no one ever helped me hold?

This kind of reframe is not just cognitive. It's somatic. Emotional. Spiritual.

It takes time. It takes practice. It takes unlearning generations of messaging that said your dignity was something you had to hustle for. But every small act of self-trust chips away at that myth. Every time you choose rest without guilt. Every time you show up imperfect and still feel worthy. Every time you speak kindly to yourself even when you fall short. That is a reclamation.

And sometimes, the shift happens in unexpected ways. A moment of stillness where you don't feel the need to explain. A conversation where you let yourself be honest. A day when you don't do anything remarkable and yet don't feel like a failure. Those are the milestones that matter. Not because they're dramatic, but because they point to a deeper truth: that you're no longer basing your worth on what you do, but on who you are.

Enough without earning it doesn't mean abandoning accountability. It means being accountable to your *wholeness*, not just your output. It means honoring your capacity without measuring it against someone else's expectations. It means choosing to believe that your softness, your needs, your boundaries, your rest—they matter just as much as your productivity.

Because if your worth is conditional, it will always be in jeopardy. But if it's inherent, you can build a life that honors it—slowly, intentionally, on your own terms.

You don't need to become someone else to be enough. You just need to stop believing that you aren't already.

* * *

5

Emotional Capitalism

There was a time when self-worth was shaped quietly—by relationships, by reflection, by the rhythms of daily life. It wasn't something you curated. It wasn't something you sold. It wasn't something you quantified. But somewhere in the last two decades, that changed. In a world increasingly driven by digital visibility, selfhood itself has become a kind of currency. Not just what you do, but who you are—or more precisely, how who you are is seen—has been folded into a vast, unrelenting marketplace.

This is emotional capitalism. A system where your inner life becomes part of your outer value. Where authenticity is content. Where vulnerability becomes strategy. Where personal growth gets measured in likes, shares, and engagement metrics. Where even rest, healing, and self-acceptance are packaged, branded, and sold back to you as lifestyle choices.

At the heart of emotional capitalism is a quiet transaction: if you express yourself in the right way, if you share your story artfully, if you let the world in just enough to be palatable but not so much as to make people uncomfortable—you'll be rewarded. Not just with attention, but with a kind of symbolic worth. You'll feel like you matter.

But that sense of mattering is fragile. It depends on visibility. On resonance. On being received well. And when it fades—when your post doesn't land, your follower count drops, your work goes unnoticed—you don't just feel overlooked. You feel unworthy.

This chapter is about the way that capitalism has crept into our most intimate spaces—not through money alone, but through metrics, visibility, and performance. It's about how we've come to equate being seen with being valued, and how that link can quietly distort our relationship to ourselves.

We'll explore the rise of personal branding as identity, the neurochemical traps of social media, the feedback loops that turn external validation into internal truth, and most importantly, the work of reclaiming your inner compass—so that your sense of self is no longer up for auction.

The Commodification of the Self

We used to ask, *Who am I?*—now we're trained to ask, *How do I appear?*

That shift might sound subtle, but it changes everything. In a culture where identity is increasingly shaped in public, being a person has become inseparable from being a product. We aren't just existing. We're curating. We're framing. We're performing versions of ourselves that are digestible, desirable, and monetizable. And often, we don't even realize we're doing it. The lines have blurred so thoroughly that branding feels like self-expression. Marketing feels like empowerment. Monetization feels like meaning.

This is the commodification of the self: the process by which our personality, our story, our presence—our very *being*—is packaged and presented as something to be consumed.

It's not just influencers and entrepreneurs who fall into this pattern. It's all of us. The therapist posting carousel tips. The academic tweeting insights in threads. The friend who filters every experience through a caption. The parent who crafts their child's image online. The nonprofit worker navigating how to show up authentically while staying "on message." It's woven into our platforms, our language, our livelihoods. And because it's everywhere, we rarely question what it's doing to us.

At first, it feels empowering. You get to define your voice. Share your truth. Reach people. Maybe even build something meaningful. But over time, something changes. You start noticing which parts of you get the most attention. You start editing your expression based on engagement. You catch yourself withholding nuance because it doesn't land well. You simplify your story for clarity. You polish your pain for impact. And slowly, you stop asking what's true and start asking what works.

It's not that you're lying. You're just adjusting. But each adjustment takes you a little further from yourself.

And it adds up.

You become fluent in performative vulnerability. You learn how to be just raw enough to seem real, just polished enough to stay aspirational. You develop a rhythm—a brand cadence. And eventually, even your silence starts to feel strategic. You're no longer just living. You're managing a feed.

For those with marginalized identities, this performance becomes even more layered. You're not just sharing—you're translating. Navigating palatability, tone, safety. You're aware that your image can open doors or close them. That being too real might cost you your job, your funding, your community. So you shape-shift. You "build your platform." You become visible in a way that feels empowering on the surface, but quietly demands conformity underneath.

And here's the kicker: this dynamic doesn't feel like coercion. It feels like opportunity.

That's what makes it so effective. Emotional capitalism doesn't force you to sell yourself. It simply rewards you for doing so. It hands you a toolkit—platforms, aesthetics, algorithms—and says, "Be yourself, but make it compelling." Be authentic, but make sure your authenticity performs well. Be vulnerable, but be strategic about it. Share, but remember your audience.

And if you're successful at it, the system rewards you—with visibility, with affirmation, maybe even with money. But that reward is also a leash. Because the moment you stop producing, the moment you get quiet, the moment you become less marketable, the rewards disappear. And so you stay in the loop. You keep curating. You keep posting. You keep tending to the version of you that performs well.

The cost of this loop is rarely acknowledged. It's the erosion of interiority. The quiet death of the unshared self. The part of you that exists without applause, without framing, without utility. That part gets smaller. Not because you don't value it—but because the world doesn't reward it.

So what does it look like to resist this? To decommodify the self?

It starts with privacy. With reclaiming spaces that aren't for public consumption. With holding parts of your life—not because they're shameful or unworthy—but because they're sacred. Because they don't need to be understood, liked, or monetized to matter.

It looks like asking: If no one saw this, would I still want it? If it got zero engagement, would it still feel meaningful? If I wasn't performing for anyone, who would I be?

It looks like refusing to let your selfhood be flattened into a narrative. It looks like honoring your complexity, even when it doesn't perform well. It looks like being a person—not a product, not a brand, not a message.

Because you are not your platform. You are not your engagement. You are not a content strategy.

You are a person with a rich interior life, a messy emotional landscape, a changing, evolving self. And that self does not exist to be marketed. It exists to be lived.

Likes, Follows, and Phantom Validation

It happens fast. You post something—a thought, a picture, a story, a piece of yourself. You wait. The first few likes come in. Someone shares it. A friend comments. Dopamine hits, subtle but real. For a moment, you feel seen. Affirmed. Connected. But as quickly as it arrives, the feeling fades. And what lingers is not peace, but a new kind of hunger: the need to keep it going.

This is the phantom validation loop. A cycle of external reinforcement that mimics belonging without ever quite delivering it. It feels like connection, but it's not the kind that anchors. It's light, quick, performative. And it's everywhere. Social media platforms are built on it—engineered to trigger the brain's reward system, to create microbursts of approval that keep you coming back for more. The goal isn't depth. It's engagement. Not resonance, but reaction.

We call it feedback, but it's not really about feedback. It's about presence.

Attention. Proof that you exist. In a world that's moving fast and rarely still, a like can feel like a lifeline. A notification, a small tap on the shoulder saying: we see you. You matter. Keep going.

But what no one tells you is that this kind of validation, once it becomes habitual, starts to replace something deeper: your own internal sense of worth.

And once that shift happens, it's hard to get back.

Because phantom validation is tricky. It doesn't feel like manipulation. It feels like connection. But it's connection stripped of context. People responding to a moment, a version, a fragment of you. They see the post, not the process. They react to the highlight, not the history. And so the response feels good—but never quite whole.

You notice it in small ways. You start tailoring what you share to what performs well. You hesitate before posting something that feels too raw, too quiet, too nuanced. You check your engagement metrics. You reread your captions. You feel disappointed when something doesn't land. You tell yourself it's no big deal—but it still gets under your skin. The silence feels louder than it should.

This isn't vanity. It's neurobiology. Social platforms are designed to exploit one of the most basic human needs: to belong. And they do it well. They know how to activate the brain's reward system. They know how to keep you chasing the next spike of affirmation. And they know that if they can tie your identity to that chase, you'll stay loyal to the loop.

But the loop has a cost. Over time, it alters the way you think about self-expression. Instead of asking, *What's true for me?* you start asking, *What will people respond to?* Instead of sharing from the inside out, you start calibrating from the outside in. You don't just present your thoughts—you market them. You don't just express your emotions—you package them. And you don't just receive feedback—you internalize it as evidence of your value.

This kind of reinforcement system doesn't just flatten identity—it fragments it. You start to develop a version of yourself that exists purely for external consumption. A persona built on resonance, stripped of friction. And the more successful that persona becomes, the more trapped you feel by it. Because now there's something to maintain. A version of yourself that people expect. A digital self that gets more feedback than the real one.

And the real one? The self that's quiet, uncertain, unpolished, and alive? That version gets pushed further into the background.

The long-term effect of this loop is a disconnection from internal validation. You forget how to feel confident without applause. You forget how to feel creative without comments. You forget how to feel real without reflection. And in moments of stillness, you feel hollow—not because you're broken, but because your nervous system has been conditioned to outsource affirmation.

So how do we break the loop?

The first step is recognition. To name what's happening. To admit the role that feedback has started to play in your emotional ecosystem. Not with shame, but with clarity. You are not weak for wanting to be seen. You are not shallow for enjoying resonance. But you are vulnerable to systems that monetize that need.

The second step is reclamation. Creating small moments where your worth isn't measured. Writing something without posting it. Creating without tracking performance. Speaking without watching yourself. Letting something exist for your eyes only. These moments are powerful not because they're private—but because they're unscored. They remind you what it feels like to belong to yourself.

And the third step is reintegration. Learning to carry both truths: that visibility can be meaningful, and that it is not necessary for worth. That feedback can feel good, and that your value is not dependent on it. That you can engage with the world—and still be sovereign within it.

The goal isn't to withdraw. It's to untangle. To separate the dopamine hit from the identity. To engage with platforms without making them the mirror for your soul.

Because you are not your notifications. You are not your follower count. You are not how well your story lands.

You are a full, feeling human being. And your need to be seen is real—but it doesn't have to be filled by a machine that profits from your insecurity.

When you learn to validate yourself from within, the feedback loop loses its grip. And what remains is something quieter, steadier, and far more sustainable: a sense of self that doesn't flicker with the algorithm.

When Feedback Becomes Self-Worth

For most of human history, our sense of value was shaped slowly—through relationships, through community, through the long arc of consistent presence. People knew us over time. They saw our complexity. They witnessed our growth, our pain, our becoming. And they didn't just respond to us; they held us. That kind of mirroring, while imperfect, helped build a sense of self that was relational but grounded. It was responsive, not reactive.

Today, that process is being replaced by something much faster, and much thinner: feedback.

Instant, abundant, shallow feedback. Comments, likes, shares, emojis. Opinions dressed up as connection. And in a world that often leaves us starved for reflection, we begin to mistake feedback for truth. For value. For identity.

And when that happens—when feedback becomes self-worth—we find ourselves living for reflection instead of inhabiting reality.

This shift is subtle, but its effects run deep. You might start checking your posts compulsively. You might replay conversations in your head based on someone's facial reaction. You might feel elated when something you say gets positive affirmation—and hollow when it doesn't. You start to track your own life not by how it feels, but by how it's received.

And when something is received well, you feel a surge of meaning. When it isn't, you start to question your judgment. Your taste. Your clarity. Your voice.

That's not sensitivity—it's displacement. Your sense of self has migrated outside your own body. Now you live in the eyes of others. And every moment becomes a referendum.

This isn't just about social media. It shows up in work, relationships, family. It's the partner who defines their worth by how needed they are. The student who can't feel good about an idea until it's praised. The professional who only feels capable when they're constantly producing. The creator who feels invisible unless their work is affirmed.

We learn this early. For many of us, feedback was the only form of love that felt safe. We weren't held consistently—we were evaluated. Graded. Judged. Praised for success, withdrawn from when we struggled. Some of us were only touched when we achieved. Only noticed when we performed. Only validated when we shaped ourselves into what others wanted.

So we adapted. We tuned our nervous systems to external cues. We listened for tone, for mood, for subtext. We became fluent in micro-adjustments. We got good at reading the room—and in the process, we lost fluency in our own feelings.

When we internalize this dynamic, we become experts at managing perception—and amateurs at self-trust.

And then adulthood arrives, and we're expected to know who we are.

But we don't. We know who we are *to others.* We know who we are *in performance.* We know how to generate feedback. But we don't know how to hear ourselves in the quiet. We don't know how to hold our truths when they're not mirrored. We don't know how to believe we matter without proof.

That absence can feel like a kind of emotional vertigo. If no one responds, do I still exist? If I'm not praised, am I still doing well? If I'm not affirmed, can I still feel right inside?

When self-worth depends on feedback, every silence becomes a threat. Every lack of response becomes personal. Every pause feels like abandonment.

And so we keep performing. We keep curating. We keep seeking validation not because we're shallow, but because the stakes feel existential. We think we're looking for feedback—but we're actually looking for ourselves.

So how do we find our way back?

The work starts with slowing down. With noticing the moments where you reach for external cues before checking your internal ones. With asking, gently: What do I feel about this—before anyone else weighs in? Do I like this? Do I believe this? Do I want this?

At first, the answers may feel distant. That's okay. You're not building a new self—you're uncovering an old one. The one that existed before it was shaped for consumption.

It also means recognizing the difference between connection and measurement. Real connection is relational, not transactional. It's not about affirmation. It's about resonance. It doesn't always feel validating. Sometimes it's challenging. Sometimes it's quiet. But it's steady. Grounded. Human.

Measurement, on the other hand, reduces your value to a score. How many views. How much praise. How quickly it landed. That kind of feedback isn't always harmful—but it's not always meaningful. And it should never be the foundation of your identity.

To disentangle self-worth from feedback is to reestablish an inner authority. It's the decision to trust your own resonance, even when it's not mirrored. To define your own metrics. To say, I know what feels true—not because someone clapped for it, but because I can feel it in my body.

And over time, that authority becomes freedom. The freedom to create without panic. To speak without self-editing. To rest without justification. To show up without apology.

You are not a project to be evaluated. You are a person to be known—first by yourself, then by others.

The truth is: feedback isn't bad. We need reflection. We grow through dialogue. But when your worth depends on constant reflection, you become a mirror instead of a self.

And you deserve more than that. You deserve to know your worth in silence. In stillness. In solitude. Because that's where real selfhood is forged—not in applause, but in the ability to stand in your truth, with or without an audience.

Breaking the Loop

There's a moment—usually quiet, often private—when you realize you can't keep doing it. The constant performing. The reaching. The measuring. The way your moods have started to rise and fall with feedback. The way you're always watching yourself from the outside. The way your sense of worth has become a score you can never quite reach. It's not a dramatic moment. It's not an announcement. It's more like a fatigue that finally registers. You're just tired. And in that tiredness, a question starts to surface: What if I don't want to live like this anymore?

Breaking the loop doesn't begin with a grand gesture. It begins with that question.

Because the loop—this system of performance, feedback, comparison, and self-surveillance—only works if you keep feeding it. If you keep posting, responding, refining, anticipating. If you keep outsourcing your self-concept to whoever happens to be watching. If you keep pretending you're okay with being reduced to a brand of yourself.

It keeps you busy. It keeps you visible. But it doesn't keep you whole.

So the work of breaking the loop is, at its core, the work of wholeness. Reintegrating the parts of you that have been edited out. Reclaiming the moments that don't perform well. Learning to value the experiences that aren't story-ready. Letting your inner world matter more than your public one.

This takes time. It takes practice. And at first, it feels like losing something. If you've spent years tying your sense of value to visibility, then stepping back will feel like erasure. You may feel less real. Less relevant. Less alive.

That's not a sign you're doing it wrong. It's a sign you're detaching from the machinery.

You will be tempted to go back. Especially in moments of loneliness, doubt, or invisibility. The loop promises quick relief. A post, a reply, a burst of affirmation. But over time, you'll begin to recognize the difference between relief and restoration. One keeps you hungry. The other feeds you.

To break the loop, you have to stop negotiating your self-worth with strangers. You have to build a quiet sanctuary inside yourself, a space that does not require applause. You have to let silence be okay. You have to let slow days count. You have to let yourself exist unscored.

That doesn't mean withdrawing completely. This isn't about disappearing. It's about showing up differently. It's about being rooted, not reactive. Intentional, not reflexive. Expressive, not performative.

It's about posting because you want to—not because you need to be seen. Speaking because something matters—not because you're managing impressions. Resting because your body asks you to—not because you've earned it.

Breaking the loop also means cultivating a different kind of mirror. Real relationships. People who hold you gently when you're not impressive. Spaces where you can bring your whole self—messy, slow, uncertain—and still feel worthy. It means finding or creating environments where your presence is enough, and where value is not a transaction.

And it means redefining success. Not as reach, not as resonance, but as alignment. Does this feel like me? Am I proud of how I showed up, even if no one claps? Would I still stand by this if it got no response?

When that becomes your metric, you begin to live from the inside out.

Of course, this is not a one-time shift. The loop is seductive. It will always offer you shortcuts to feeling okay. But those shortcuts are hollow. They can't hold you through real pain. They can't answer your deeper questions. They can't love you back.

Only you can do that.

And maybe that's the most radical thing: to become someone who can hold their own worth. To build a self that is not a brand. To live a life that doesn't require constant validation to feel real.

Because at the end of the day, the most meaningful kind of visibility isn't public—it's internal. It's when you can look at yourself with clarity and care and say: I see you. I know you. I love who you are becoming.

Even when no one else is watching.

* * *

6

Good Enough Was Never the Goal

Some people are perfectionists because they want to be excellent. Others are perfectionists because they're terrified of what will happen if they're not.

This chapter is for the second group.

For the ones who can't relax until everything's in order. Who replay conversations for days. Who reread every message before sending it. Who apologize for things no one noticed. Who always feel like they're one misstep away from being exposed. Not because they crave achievement—but because they fear rejection. Or judgment. Or chaos. Or abandonment.

Perfectionism, in this context, isn't about pride. It's about protection. A defense strategy so deeply wired that it no longer feels like strategy. It feels like reality. Like the only way to be safe in the world is to be error-free. The only way to be lovable is to be impressive. The only way to avoid collapse is to control every variable.

That's why telling a perfectionist to "just let go" doesn't work. It misses the point. It assumes perfectionism is a lifestyle choice—when for many, it's a survival mechanism.

And it usually starts early.

Children don't wake up one day and decide they need to be perfect. They learn it. Through the subtle rewards of praise. Through the sharp edges of criticism. Through homes where mistakes weren't tolerated. Through classrooms where being right earned belonging. Through relationships where love came with expectations. Through systems that made some identities feel like they had to be twice as good to be seen as enough.

What begins as effort becomes identity. And once it's part of who you are, letting it go feels like failure. Or worse—like vulnerability.

This chapter is about that kind of perfectionism. The kind that comes from fear, not ego. The kind that makes you harder on yourself than anyone else would ever dare to be. The kind that wears a mask of competence, but underneath is exhausted, brittle, and quietly terrified.

We'll explore how perfectionism becomes a way to feel safe, why shame and error are so deeply linked for some people, how social identity complicates the pressure to get things right, and what it actually looks like to stop performing without losing your sense of worth.

Because good enough was never the goal. It was survival. And the moment you realize that, you can begin the work of choosing something different—not perfection, not performance, but freedom.

The Fantasy of Safety Through Perfection

There's a reason perfectionism feels non-negotiable for so many people. It isn't just about impressing others. It's about managing fear. Fear of being misunderstood. Fear of letting someone down. Fear of being punished, abandoned, or made small. Perfectionism, at its core, is a fantasy of safety. It promises that if you can just do everything right, you'll be protected—from shame, from scrutiny, from being hurt in the ways you've been hurt before.

And for a while, it works. That's the dangerous part. There's a short-term payoff. You get praised. You avoid conflict. You earn trust. You come across as capable, reliable, competent. People admire your work ethic. They respect your precision. You feel useful. Maybe even powerful. But underneath the surface, something else is happening: you begin to believe that this version of yourself—the controlled, polished, unfailing version—is the only one worthy of being seen.

That's not confidence. That's armor.

Many perfectionists learned early on that love could be lost. That approval could be withdrawn. That attention was tied to performance. Maybe you had caregivers who were harsh or critical. Maybe you had to be the adult in a chaotic household. Maybe your mistakes were met with anger. Maybe your accomplishments were the only thing that made you visible. Maybe you had to work harder than your peers just to be taken seriously. Whatever the story, the message was clear: you are safest when you are perfect.

So you adapted. You became vigilant. You anticipated needs before anyone said them. You double-checked everything. You tried to be flawless. And each time it worked—each time your perfection kept you out of trouble, or won someone's praise—it reinforced the strategy.

But over time, the cost grows.

You stop trusting your instincts. You hesitate to take risks. You delay creative projects out of fear they won't be good enough. You avoid emotional intimacy because you can't control how others will respond to the real you. You micromanage your life—and often, the lives of others. You become reactive to minor mistakes. You burn out. But instead of resting, you self-criticize. You tell yourself you should be stronger, sharper, more disciplined. You believe the lie that exhaustion is a personal failure, not a system failure.

And the worst part? You start to lose track of what you actually want. Because everything becomes about maintaining the illusion. You don't just strive—you surveil. Every decision is calculated. Every expression is edited. You don't show up—you manage perception. And little by little, you begin to disappear under the weight of your own performance.

This is the trap of perfectionism as safety: it gives you just enough validation to stay committed, but never enough peace to feel free.

Even when people tell you you're doing great, it doesn't land. You assume they don't see the full picture. You worry they've been fooled by your mask. You're waiting for the other shoe to drop—for someone to notice the flaw you've been trying to hide. And because you've attached your worth to your image, any crack in that image feels catastrophic. A small mistake becomes a threat. A minor correction feels like rejection. A bad day means you're falling apart.

This is not a mindset problem. It's a trauma pattern.

The nervous system doesn't forget what it had to do to feel safe. And if you had to be perfect to stay loved, protected, or noticed, then letting go of that strategy feels like walking into danger. Not emotional discomfort—actual danger. That's why perfectionists often resist help. Why they struggle to delegate. Why they keep raising the bar. The body doesn't know you're no longer in that old environment. It's still bracing for impact.

So what's the way out?

It's not abandoning high standards. It's shifting the reason you hold them. Perfectionism says: I have to get it exactly right or something bad will happen. Excellence says: I want to do this well because it matters to me. One is rooted in fear. The other is rooted in care.

The work begins with curiosity. Noticing when perfectionism kicks in. Tracking what it's trying to protect you from. Asking: What am I afraid will happen if I let this be imperfect? What does this mistake say about me, in my own mind? Whose voice do I hear when I criticize myself?

And then—gently—begin to interrupt the cycle. Let something be 90 percent done instead of 100. Send the email without rereading it five times. Let someone see your mess. Rest before you're finished. Accept praise without disclaimers. Let people down, gently and respectfully, and notice that the world doesn't collapse.

These small acts of imperfection are not failures. They're resistance. They're repair. They're proof that your safety no longer depends on being flawless. And each time you survive them, your nervous system begins to learn a new story: I can be loved and imperfect. I can be safe and unfinished. I can make mistakes and still be whole.

That's the real fantasy worth building—not safety through perfection, but safety through self-trust.

Shame, Mistakes, and the Fear of Disappointment

For some people, a mistake is a problem to be solved. For others, it's a threat to their sense of self. The difference is rarely about ego. More often, it's about shame. When you carry the belief—often unspoken, always heavy—that to mess up is to be unworthy, then even small errors can feel like confirmation of your deepest fear: that you are fundamentally not enough.

This isn't about being overly sensitive. It's about emotional conditioning. Many of us were raised in environments where mistakes weren't treated as learning opportunities but as breaches of character. Maybe you were scolded harshly for small things. Maybe you were mocked or shamed for not knowing something. Maybe you learned that competence was the only path to being treated with respect—or to being noticed at all.

Over time, mistakes stopped being moments. They became evidence. Evidence that you were unprepared, unworthy, a burden, a fraud. And because you didn't want to feel those things—or because you feared what would happen if others saw you that way—you started preempting mistakes before they could happen. You started rehearsing everything. You built your personality around reliability, control, and anticipation.

And when something still slipped through—because something always does—the shame hit like a tidal wave.

This is the difference between guilt and shame. Guilt says, *I did something wrong.* Shame says, *I am something wrong.* And perfectionism, when driven by shame, isn't about high standards. It's about emotional survival. If I never mess up, I won't feel that pain. If I never disappoint anyone, I'll stay safe.

But it doesn't work. Because no matter how hard you try, mistakes still happen. You forget the appointment. You miss the deadline. You say the wrong thing. You drop the ball. And when it happens, the voice in your head doesn't just say, *That was unfortunate.* It says, *You ruined everything. You always do this. Everyone's going to see who you really are.*

That voice didn't come from nowhere.

It came from early experiences where errors weren't just noticed—they were punished. Where disappointment wasn't met with care—it was met with distance. Where being wrong meant being unworthy of kindness. For some, this came from family. For others, it came from school, from religion, from cultural scripts that equated morality with flawlessness.

And so now, in adulthood, the emotional weight of a mistake feels disproportionate to the moment itself. You're not just worried about fixing the problem. You're flooded with self-doubt. You spiral. You ruminate. You apologize excessively. You brace for backlash, even when it's not coming.

This spiral doesn't just exhaust you—it shrinks you. You take fewer risks. You become hypervigilant in relationships. You avoid projects where the outcome is uncertain. You opt for what's familiar, even when it doesn't align with who you're becoming.

But here's the truth: making mistakes is not the problem. Equating mistakes with moral failure is.

We live in a culture that idolizes the idea of being "unproblematic." The polished brand. The clean track record. The resume that never stumbles. But real life is messy. And growth always leaves a trace. If you're living fully, you're going to get it wrong sometimes. You're going to misread situations, misjudge timing, misplace trust. That's not a flaw in your character. That's part of the deal.

What matters is what happens next.

When you can learn to hold your own mistakes with care instead of condemnation, everything changes. You stop hiding. You stop overcorrecting. You start repairing instead of retreating. You stop expecting yourself to be perfect, and you start expecting yourself to be responsible. Those aren't the same thing. One comes from fear. The other comes from integrity.

The path to that shift starts with unpacking your internal response. When shame hits, pause and name it. *This feels bigger than it is. This is shame, not truth.* Ask yourself: What story is my brain telling me right now? Whose voice does it sound like? Is it kind? Is it accurate? Is it helpful?

Then ask: What would I say to someone I love if they made this exact mistake?

The answers are usually gentle, reasonable, human. That's the voice you're trying to reclaim. Not to excuse errors, but to respond to them with the kind of grounded compassion that allows for growth.

It also helps to separate *impact* from *identity*. You can acknowledge harm without collapsing into self-loathing. You can take responsibility without erasing your worth. You can say, *I was wrong* without believing *I am wrong*.

This is especially important in relationships. People who fear disappointment often over-apologize or shut down entirely. But healthy relationships aren't built on perfection. They're built on repair. When you own your mistake clearly and calmly—without spiraling—you make space for trust, not just performance.

And the more often you survive that process, the more your nervous system begins to believe that mistakes are not existential threats. They're part of the rhythm of being alive.

Over time, something subtle but profound happens: you stop fearing the moment when things go wrong. You stop bracing for judgment. You start trusting your ability to navigate difficulty. And that, more than any performance of flawlessness, is what creates real emotional security.

Because worthiness isn't about never disappointing others. It's about knowing that even when you do, you're still enough. You're still worthy of love, of care, of second chances.

Gender, Race, and the Performance of Competence

Perfectionism is never just a personality quirk. It's shaped by culture, identity, and survival. And for many people—especially those navigating systems shaped by whiteness, patriarchy, or class hierarchy—perfectionism isn't just internal pressure. It's a response to external surveillance. The world is watching. The rules are uneven. The stakes are higher. So the performance becomes tighter. Cleaner. Less forgiving.

Let's name it clearly: not everyone is allowed to make mistakes the same way.

If you're a woman, especially in professional or academic spaces, you're expected to be warm but not too emotional, competent but not aggressive, collaborative but still individually accountable. You're taught to anticipate everyone's needs without asking for too much in return. And when you succeed, it's often attributed to charm or luck—while your failures are treated as confirmation that you weren't ready to begin with.

So you learn to be impeccable.

You work twice as hard to be seen as half as prepared. You over-prepare for meetings. You edit your emails six times. You take on extra emotional labor. You smooth out your opinions to avoid conflict. You carry the team and deflect credit. You do everything right—and still wonder if it will be enough.

Now add race.

Black professionals, for example, often grow up knowing that their mistakes won't be interpreted as individual lapses—they'll be seen as representative. You're not just carrying your own reputation. You're carrying the expectations of how your entire group will be judged. That's not just unfair—it's dehumanizing. And it creates a pressure to be perfect that's not optional. It's protective.

If you're Latina, Asian, Indigenous, Middle Eastern—each identity comes with its own set of assumptions to fight against. Maybe you're exoticized, dismissed, expected to be deferential or "grateful." Maybe your intelligence is questioned, your accent mocked, your tone policed. So you stay vigilant. You outperform. You over-articulate. You become fluent in the cultural code-switching required to be read as credible.

And then there's queerness, disability, neurodivergence. Each with its own terrain of invalidation. Each with its own pressures to mask, to moderate, to prove your legitimacy over and over again. The performance of competence becomes armor—and it has to be. Because the minute you falter, the doubts people already had about you come rushing in.

This isn't imagined. It's lived. And it leaves a mark.

Even in spaces that claim to be progressive or inclusive, these dynamics persist. The internal pressure to be flawless isn't just self-generated. It's a reflection of external scrutiny. You're not trying to be perfect because you're arrogant. You're trying to be bulletproof.

That changes the conversation.

Because when we frame perfectionism as a personal flaw, we ignore the systems that reward it unevenly. We put the burden on individuals to "just relax" without addressing why some people never had the luxury to be relaxed in the first place. We miss the context that makes perfectionism make sense.

So let's talk about what it actually feels like.

It feels like being in a constant state of performance. Like knowing you'll be judged not just for what you do, but for how you do it. Like learning that being exceptional isn't optional—it's the baseline. Like navigating spaces where your peers are allowed to be average, but you're expected to be extraordinary just to be taken seriously.

It feels like hiding your exhaustion. Like avoiding vulnerability. Like never asking for help, because help might be interpreted as incompetence. Like downplaying your achievements so you're not seen as arrogant—but also never making a mistake, because then you're seen as incompetent.

It's not sustainable. And it's not fair. But it's real. And it shapes everything.

So what's the alternative? Certainly not asking people to stop protecting themselves in environments that still penalize difference. The goal isn't to shame people out of perfectionism. It's to name the context clearly, so we can begin to hold it differently.

One place to start is by distinguishing between survival performance and authentic excellence. Are you striving because it's aligned with your values—or because you're afraid of being dismissed, overlooked, or harmed? Are you pushing yourself because you're inspired—or because you've internalized a belief that one misstep will cost you everything?

This awareness doesn't fix the systems. But it restores your agency. It allows you to make conscious choices about how much of yourself to perform, how often to code-switch, when to challenge the script and when to protect your peace.

And when safe spaces do exist—where your whole self is welcome—you can start practicing what it means to be imperfect *and* respected. To ask for support without fear. To rest without guilt. To let your humanity show without bracing for judgment.

That kind of healing isn't just personal. It's political. Every time someone from a marginalized identity lets themselves be complex, unfinished, or honest, it chips away at the myth that we only matter when we're perfect.

We don't need more flawless performances. We need more space for real people—messy, smart, feeling, tired, brilliant, whole.

The Liberation of Messiness

There comes a point in a perfectionist's life—sometimes after a crisis, sometimes just a quiet moment of exhaustion—when they realize they're holding themselves hostage. Not because they want to. But because somewhere along the way, they mistook flawlessness for worth. Now, every undone task feels like a moral failure. Every awkward moment becomes a character indictment. Every vulnerability feels like danger. And it's not that they don't want freedom. It's that freedom feels like risk.

But here's the shift: messiness is not collapse. It's contact. It's reality. It's the part of life that doesn't fit in your planner but still belongs to you.

To understand the liberation of messiness, we have to start with what mess actually is.

Mess is the email you didn't answer because your brain was fogged out with grief. It's the conversation you fumbled because you were exhausted, overstimulated, or afraid. It's the version of your work that's 80% done but still honest. It's the dishes in the sink and the thoughts you can't quite articulate and the emotional responses that come before you're ready to explain them.

Mess is life before it's edited.

And it matters because the version of ourselves we perform for the world—the one that's polished, presentable, and easily digested—is never the full story. We all carry doubt. We all lose steam. We all have days where we get it wrong. The difference is that some of us have been taught that showing those parts makes us unworthy.

So we hide them. We mask. We hustle. We "fix" ourselves before anyone notices. And then we feel disconnected—lonely, burned out, unseen—and don't understand why.

But there's no intimacy without mess. No creativity. No rest. No real joy.

Because all those things require space to be unpolished. They require room to be fully human.

The liberation begins when we stop organizing our lives around control and begin organizing them around permission.

Permission to not know yet. To try and miss the mark. To rest before it's urgent. To speak even if your voice shakes. To be a whole human being without waiting for perfection.

This isn't chaos. It's clarity. When you allow mess, you make space for real choices. You stop reacting and start responding. You learn to sit with tension instead of rushing to resolve it. You recognize that discomfort isn't failure—it's feedback.

And the more you practice, the less afraid you become.

You let your home reflect your real energy. You create without needing it to be brilliant. You show up to the meeting as you are—not as the version of you you rehearsed all night. You say, "I don't know" without shame. You admit when you're not at your best—and don't spiral.

This doesn't mean you give up on growth. It means you stop performing health. You stop confusing control with maturity. You stop believing that your value is something you have to maintain, polish, or earn.

It also means rethinking accountability.

Messiness doesn't absolve us of responsibility—it deepens it. When we're no longer busy defending a façade, we can actually engage with the impact of our actions. We can own harm, repair, listen, and learn. Not because we're trying to preserve an image—but because we care about being in real relationship.

That's the paradox: messiness makes us more accountable, not less. Because it puts us in contact with reality. With others. With ourselves.

In practice, this often starts small. You let someone see your house when it's not clean. You show up to therapy and say, "I'm not sure where to start." You send the project draft even though it feels unfinished. You share a feeling before it's perfectly formed. You allow a pause in a conversation without rushing to fill it.

Each of these moments creates a micro-fissure in the perfectionist shell.

And each fissure is an opening—for relief, for truth, for connection.

Because what you'll find, again and again, is that people are more drawn to your wholeness than your polish. They're moved by your honesty. They're softened by your softness. They're inspired not by your control, but by your courage to be real.

And most importantly, you begin to trust yourself. Not the version of you who always gets it right. But the version who can stay present when things go sideways. Who can hold contradiction. Who can be honest even when it's inconvenient.

That version isn't fragile. It's resilient. Because it's rooted in reality. And reality, however messy, is the only place we can actually belong.

So here's the invitation: stop asking yourself to be perfect. Start asking yourself to be present. Let your life be a little messy. Let your self-worth be sturdy enough to survive a bad day, an awkward moment, an unmet expectation.

Because freedom isn't found in getting it all right.

It's found in being able to get it wrong—and still know you're enough.

* * *

7

The Problem Isn't Motivation

If you've ever stared at a task for hours, or days, or weeks—wanting to do it, knowing you should do it, but still not doing it—you're not alone. And more importantly, you're not broken. Because what looks like a motivation problem is almost never about motivation at all. It's usually about fear. Or overwhelm. Or shame. Or perfectionism. Or the subtle, persistent belief that no matter what you do, it won't be enough.

This chapter is about that kind of paralysis. The kind where your to-do list starts to feel like a character judgment. Where every delay feels like failure. Where even small tasks feel enormous. And instead of naming what's really happening, you tell yourself the same story you've heard all your life: You're lazy. You lack discipline. You need to try harder.

But that story is a lie. One we've all been fed in a culture that mistakes chronic stress for personal weakness, and self-judgment for self-control.

We're going to challenge that. Because what we call procrastination is rarely a moral failure. It's often an emotional response. And until we treat it as such, we stay trapped—shaming ourselves for what is, in fact, a nervous system trying to protect us.

Most people don't avoid tasks because they don't care. They avoid tasks because those tasks are loaded—with pressure, with uncertainty, with the possibility of disappointment. Or because the environment around the task is unsafe. Or because they've associated productivity with conditional worth. Or because they're afraid that finishing the task won't bring relief, only the next demand.

So the body resists. Not because it's lazy. But because it's wise.

This is especially true for people with trauma histories, chronic stress, ADHD, depression, anxiety—any context in which executive functioning is impacted. When your brain is in survival mode, prioritizing, sequencing, initiating, and completing tasks aren't just difficult—they can feel physiologically impossible. Not because you're unmotivated. Because you're dysregulated.

And no amount of self-punishment solves dysregulation.

So in this chapter, we'll break the myth of lazy people. We'll look at how the nervous system responds to threat and how that translates into task aversion. We'll unpack the shame-procrastination loop and why it keeps us stuck. And we'll explore a different approach to momentum—one rooted in compassion, not criticism.

Because motivation isn't the fuel for action. It's the result of connection. And when you stop asking yourself to perform your way out of paralysis, and start listening to what the resistance is actually saying, you create the conditions for movement that doesn't cost your dignity.

The Myth of Lazy People

We love to talk about lazy people. The ones who can't get it together. The ones who miss deadlines, skip steps, let opportunities pass. We describe them as if they're flawed—unmotivated, irresponsible, selfish, weak. We talk about them with a mix of contempt and pity. And sometimes, we talk about ourselves that way.

But here's the truth: the concept of laziness is a cultural fantasy.

It gives us a simple label for something that is almost never simple. It lets us collapse complex internal realities into a single accusation. And in doing so, it hides what's really happening.

Because in over a decade of studying human behavior, I've never met a person who was truly lazy. I've met people who are afraid. People who are dysregulated. People who are overwhelmed, grieving, overworked, undersupported, unsure of where to begin. I've met people whose perfectionism shuts them down before they can even start. People who can't initiate tasks because their nervous system has been running on fumes for years. People whose entire lives have been shaped by the belief that their value depends on being useful.

And when those people freeze, when they delay, when they can't muster the energy to "just do it," they're not opting out. They're maxed out. But instead of recognizing that, they internalize the myth: I must be lazy. And that story becomes part of their identity.

It's a cruel narrative. And it's especially punishing for those whose experiences are already misunderstood. Neurodivergent people are constantly told they're lazy, when what they're really dealing with is executive dysfunction. People with depression hear the same thing, when their cognitive and emotional resources are already strained to the edge. Trauma survivors are labeled as unmotivated, when their nervous systems are still bracing for danger. Even highly accomplished people who hit periods of burnout or paralysis often turn on themselves, convinced their inability to function must reflect a moral flaw.

But laziness, as a character trait, doesn't hold up under scrutiny. If you dig beneath it, you'll almost always find something else. Avoidance. Shame. Exhaustion. Fear. Sometimes defiance. Sometimes disconnection. But never nothing.

Because humans are meaning-driven creatures. We move toward what feels possible, purposeful, or safe. And when we stop moving, there's a reason.

Maybe it's because the task feels pointless—divorced from our values, imposed by someone else, or disconnected from any felt sense of impact. Maybe it's because we've learned that achievement doesn't bring peace, only more expectation. Maybe we're protecting ourselves from the vulnerability of failure. Maybe we're waiting to feel safe enough to begin. Maybe we're so accustomed to pressure that we don't know how to act without it.

The point is, none of that is laziness. It's data. It's information about how your system is responding to the world around you—and the expectations placed on you.

When we call someone lazy, we shut down that inquiry. We replace curiosity with condemnation. And we rob ourselves of the opportunity to actually understand what would help.

This matters, especially in relationships. If someone close to you seems "lazy," try asking what they're avoiding—and why. Ask what their resistance is protecting them from. Ask what they need to feel safe enough to act. You'll often find that what looks like indifference is actually a fear of failure, or a belief that their effort won't matter, or a nervous system so overwhelmed that the very idea of starting feels like drowning.

And if you're the one being hard on yourself, the same invitation applies.

Instead of saying, *I'm so lazy,* ask: *What feels impossible about this right now? What am I afraid will happen if I start? What would this task mean about me if I did it wrong—or if I did it well and nothing changed? What am I trying to protect myself from?*

These questions aren't meant to let you off the hook. They're meant to get you out of the loop. Because shame doesn't lead to momentum. It leads to shutdown. And every time you call yourself lazy, you reinforce the very paralysis you're trying to escape.

So what's the alternative?

Compassionate inquiry. Adjusting the frame from "Why can't I just do this?" to "What would make this easier to start?" Building scaffolding around the task—not just systems of organization, but systems of emotional support. Making peace with imperfect action. Learning to recognize the voice of internalized productivity culture and choosing, again and again, not to let it dictate your worth.

Because motivation isn't something you summon through force. It's something you cultivate through safety, clarity, and meaning.

And when you stop accusing yourself of being lazy, you create space for those things to emerge.

Task Aversion and the Nervous System

When people talk about procrastination, they almost always frame it as a mindset issue—something that can be fixed with better habits, more willpower, or a different morning routine. But what those conversations leave out is the body. Not the body as metaphor, but the literal, physiological system you live inside. Because more often than not, the reason we avoid tasks isn't because we don't care. It's because our nervous system is signaling danger.

To understand task aversion, we have to start with how the brain processes stress.

Your nervous system has one job above all others: keep you alive. And it's not especially concerned with accuracy—it cares about pattern recognition. It tracks the environment, scans for cues of safety or threat, and responds accordingly. When something feels threatening, your body reacts. Not when something *is* threatening, but when it *feels* like it might be. That distinction is everything.

So what happens when a task—an email, a form, a phone call, a creative project—triggers that threat response?

Your body moves into one of four states: fight, flight, freeze, or fawn. In the context of task aversion, freeze and fawn are the most common. Freeze looks like staring at your screen, unable to start. Fawn looks like immediately turning your attention to someone else's needs—cleaning the kitchen, answering someone's text, rechecking an older task—because that's safer than facing the one thing you're avoiding.

This isn't laziness. It's a system override. Your brain is perceiving the task as too much—too uncertain, too consequential, too linked to past failure or future judgment. So it says: don't move. Stay still. Postpone. Numb out. Redirect. And you obey. Not because you want to. Because in that moment, your nervous system is more persuasive than your calendar.

Sometimes the task itself is what triggers the response. A form that reminds you of bureaucracy. A call that reminds you of conflict. A document that signals exposure or critique. But often, it's not the task—it's the meaning.

You're not afraid of the spreadsheet. You're afraid of what will happen if you get it wrong. Or of what it says about you if it's not perfect. Or of the attention it might generate. Or of the outcome it might lock in.

These are emotional threats. And they light up the same systems as physical ones.

Add in a history of trauma, neurodivergence, burnout, or chronic stress, and your threshold for perceived threat lowers. Your body doesn't need much to go on. It just needs to *remember.* It needs to sense a familiar feeling—dread, pressure, judgment—and it begins to act as if it's under siege.

This is why advice like "just push through" so often backfires. If someone is already in a state of nervous system activation, pushing harder doesn't resolve the resistance. It intensifies it. And if they manage to override it temporarily, they often crash later—because the body was never actually safe.

The key is regulation, not force.

Regulation doesn't mean calming down. It means returning to a state where choice is possible. Where action doesn't feel like a threat. Where the task can be engaged without panic, collapse, or avoidance. That's the state where real productivity lives—not in the hustle of adrenaline, but in the grounded place where your system believes it's okay to try.

So how do we get there?

First: pause. Before you try to "get yourself together," notice what's happening in your body. Are you tense? Numb? Rushing? Shaky? Avoidant? Shut down? What's the first feeling that shows up when you think about the task?

Next: name it. *This feels like threat. My body is trying to protect me. This isn't defiance. It's defense.*

Then: support your system. That might mean movement. It might mean breathing in a way that signals safety. It might mean a brief connection with someone who helps you feel grounded. It might mean doing something small—*extremely* small—that reconnects you to a sense of agency. Washing a dish. Opening the document. Writing one word.

Sometimes, it means giving yourself permission not to begin until your system is ready. That's not indulgence. That's strategy. Because when your body feels safe, it stops resisting. And the task that felt impossible starts to feel accessible again.

This approach requires compassion. It requires trusting that your system is not betraying you—it's trying to help. And once you understand what it's protecting you from, you can begin to create a new relationship with the work in front of you. One where your value isn't on the line. One where your fear doesn't call the shots. One where action is an invitation, not a demand.

Over time, this changes how you move through the world. You begin to recognize the difference between resistance and avoidance. You learn to respond to the cues in your body instead of judging them. You start building scaffolding that respects your limits while still moving you forward. You stop pretending your tasks exist in a vacuum, and start acknowledging the full emotional context in which they live.

And most importantly, you stop calling yourself lazy. Because the moment you understand that task aversion is nervous system logic—not personal failure—you begin to build a life where movement is sustainable. Where effort is possible. Where progress doesn't require panic. Where you're not fighting your own body every time something hard needs doing.

The Shame-Procrastination Loop

For many people, procrastination doesn't feel like putting something off. It feels like failure in slow motion. You know the task needs doing. You feel the pressure mounting. You're fully aware that every passing day will make it harder. But instead of starting, you freeze—or distract—or do something else that feels safer. And the longer you delay, the worse you feel. Not just anxious, but ashamed.

This is the loop. And it feeds itself.

It starts with pressure. A task appears—an email, a project, a call, a decision. Maybe you don't feel ready. Maybe it's too big. Maybe it reminds you of something that went wrong before. You hesitate. That hesitation triggers discomfort. Your brain says, "You really should have started by now." You feel guilty. You try to ignore it. Guilt becomes shame. Shame becomes paralysis.

And that paralysis gets interpreted as more evidence that you're failing.

So you avoid the task longer. You criticize yourself more. And the loop tightens.

Most people think the key to breaking this cycle is motivation. But that's not how the brain works. The more shame you feel, the harder it becomes to take action. Shame doesn't activate—it immobilizes. It shrinks your sense of possibility. It turns tasks into symbols of personal inadequacy. And once that association forms, even thinking about the task triggers a stress response.

So you avoid thinking about it. You avoid opening the email. You avoid the document, the draft, the conversation. You tell yourself you'll feel better tomorrow. But tomorrow comes and you still feel like a failure. So you avoid it again. And now the task has company: anxiety, fear, dread.

The irony is that this pattern often happens to people who care deeply. People who want to do well. People who are used to being high performers. That's part of what makes the shame so toxic. You're not just delaying—you're betraying your own idea of who you're supposed to be.

And so you start negotiating with yourself. You create elaborate timelines. You bargain: "If I just focus today, I can make up for it." You set unrealistic expectations and then crash when you can't meet them. You beat yourself up, thinking that if you punish yourself hard enough, you'll finally get moving.

But punishment doesn't produce progress. It produces fear. And fear, sustained over time, turns even the simplest tasks into psychological minefields.

Cognitive behavioral theory explains this loop well. At the core is a belief—often unconscious—that completing the task will be painful. Not the task itself, but what it means. It might mean facing criticism. It might mean no longer having an excuse for failure. It might mean dealing with change or responsibility or visibility. So the brain says: better to avoid. Safer to delay.

But avoidance comes with consequences. You lose sleep. You miss opportunities. You feel out of alignment. And each consequence deepens the shame.

Eventually, the pain of avoidance outweighs the fear of action. That's when most people finally break the loop—not because they've gained clarity, but because the discomfort becomes unbearable. They act from desperation, not agency. And even when they finish the task, they don't feel proud. They feel depleted. Relieved, maybe. But not empowered.

There's another way.

It starts with dropping the narrative of laziness. With replacing judgment with inquiry. When you notice avoidance, ask: What am I afraid this task will reveal about me? What does finishing mean in my mind? What am I trying to protect myself from? What would I need to believe in order to begin?

Then: lower the barrier. Break the task into something smaller—so small it feels almost silly. Don't aim for completion. Aim for contact. Open the tab. Name the task out loud. Write one sentence. Send one line. The goal isn't to finish—it's to interrupt the freeze.

As you do this, bring in self-talk that's actually useful. Not "I should have done this sooner," but "This is hard for a reason." Not "I'm so behind," but "I'm coming back to it now." These shifts seem minor, but they recalibrate your nervous system. They signal that you're not being hunted—you're being human.

And when you inevitably feel the shame surge again, meet it. Not with denial, but with context. *This is shame. Not truth. It's a response to pressure. It's not a verdict on my worth.*

That's how the loop begins to loosen. Not through discipline alone, but through compassion. Through learning that your resistance is not disobedience—it's a flare from your internal system, asking for care.

Over time, this changes your identity. You stop seeing yourself as someone who can't follow through. You start recognizing patterns. You build systems that work with your rhythms instead of against them. You understand that productivity doesn't require perfection—it requires presence.

Most importantly, you begin to trust yourself again. Not just to act, but to return. To begin late. To move imperfectly. To hold shame when it comes, and not let it become a cage.

Because the opposite of procrastination isn't productivity. It's self-connection. And that's where momentum truly lives.

Motivation as a Byproduct, Not a Prerequisite

Most of us are taught to treat motivation like a prerequisite: a mood or state of mind we have to wait for before we begin. If you're not feeling motivated, the assumption goes, you're not ready. You need to push harder. Or trick yourself. Or wait for the right spark to arrive so you can finally get going.

But that framework is backward.

Motivation isn't what gets you started. It's what shows up once you're in motion. And more importantly, it's not a feeling you need to chase—it's a result of connection, clarity, and care. The reason so many people stay stuck is not because they lack ambition. It's because the conditions that support sustainable action have been ignored.

Think of motivation less like fuel and more like momentum. It's not about hype. It's about rhythm. And rhythm doesn't start with force. It starts with contact—with showing up to a task in small, low-pressure ways that build trust in your own system.

Let's take a closer look at why this matters.

If you've ever delayed starting something because you "just weren't in the right mindset," you know how deceptive that logic can be. Days pass. Then weeks. The pressure builds. And when you finally try to begin, it feels even harder—because now the task carries all the weight of your self-doubt. You don't just have to complete it. You have to redeem yourself for not doing it sooner.

This is where the productivity world fails us. It tells us to wait for "inspiration" or use hacks to jolt ourselves into focus. It tells us to buy the right planner, build the perfect schedule, or visualize the end goal. And when those tools don't work, it says the problem must be inside us. We lack discipline. We don't want it badly enough.

But what we often lack isn't motivation—it's safety. Or permission. Or a bridge between where we are and what we're asking ourselves to do.

So what if we stopped waiting for motivation to arrive, and started designing for engagement instead?

That means focusing on the entry point. Not the outcome. Not the full list.

Just the first moment of contact. What's the smallest possible step you can take? Something so easy it feels almost laughable. Open the doc. Type one sentence. Set a two-minute timer. Glance at the subject line. These aren't shortcuts—they're anchors. They lower the threshold. They quiet the panic. They create a beginning.

And that beginning matters. Because action generates clarity. It gives your system proof: this is safe. I can do this. I'm allowed to try. And once that permission lands, motivation starts to trickle in—not as a sudden burst, but as a shift in tone. You're no longer staring at the task from the outside. You're inside it. And inside is where flow happens.

This model also honors the role of compassion.

When you're stuck, what helps isn't a louder inner critic. It's an inner collaborator. A voice that says, "I see you. This is hard. Let's just start here." That voice doesn't let you off the hook—it just stops making the hook the point. It reframes your effort as an experiment, not a referendum on your worth.

And experiments are allowed to be messy. They're allowed to stall and start again. They're allowed to scale down. They're allowed to succeed in partial ways. That flexibility doesn't weaken discipline. It strengthens it—because it keeps the door open. You don't have to be perfect. You just have to stay in the process.

This shift also reframes success.

Instead of measuring success by what you complete, you measure it by how consistently you return. You become someone who comes back. Someone who notices resistance and meets it. Someone who lets progress look like presence, not performance.

And the more you practice that return, the more your nervous system learns that effort is not a threat. It becomes safer to act. Safer to try. Safer to continue. The loop shifts from paralysis to participation.

That's where real motivation lives. Not in the adrenaline of last-minute panic. Not in the fantasy of one perfect breakthrough. But in the steady, gentle accumulation of choices that keep you connected to your own aliveness.

So if you're waiting to feel ready, don't.

Begin where you are. Let readiness catch up to you.

* * *

8

The Inner Critic Isn't You

There's a voice in your head that narrates your failures. You know the one. It tells you you're behind. It questions your motives. It rewrites every stumble as a sign of inadequacy. It says things like: You should have done more. You always do this. You're never going to get it right. And sometimes, you believe it. Not because you want to, but because the voice feels so familiar that it's hard to imagine a version of you that doesn't include it.

But here's the truth: that voice is not you.

It might live in your head. It might sound like your own thoughts. But it's not your essence. It's not your truth. It's a structure—a learned mechanism. And you didn't invent it alone. You inherited it. From families. From schools. From institutions. From environments that rewarded obedience and punished vulnerability. From systems that taught you safety came through self-correction. That value came through control. That emotional pain should be hidden, minimized, or explained away.

The inner critic is a survival strategy dressed up as self-awareness.

And this chapter is about unraveling that. About learning where that voice came from, why it developed, and what it's trying to protect you from. Because even though the critic can feel cruel, its roots are usually in fear—not malice. Fear of abandonment. Fear of being unlovable. Fear of failure, rejection, punishment, invisibility.

So we'll begin by identifying the voice—when it shows up, what it says, and who it sounds like. Then we'll move into a trauma-informed understanding of internal criticism, using tools like Internal Family Systems (IFS) and parts theory to map how this voice functions as a protector, not a persecutor. We'll look at why harshness can feel like clarity, and how so many of us confuse self-judgment with maturity. And we'll end by exploring what it takes to build a relationship with yourself that's rooted in witnessing, not war.

Because the goal isn't to silence the inner critic by force. The goal is to disidentify from it. To recognize that you are not the voice—you are the space it moves through. You're the one who can pause, observe, respond. And in that pause, you regain the power to parent yourself differently. To shift the tone. To make space for nuance. To stop managing yourself like a threat, and start relating to yourself as someone worthy of tenderness.

You don't need to earn your way into self-compassion. You need to remember that it was always your birthright—buried beneath someone else's fear.

Identifying the Critical Voice

Before you can change your relationship with your inner critic, you have to know what you're dealing with. And not just in the abstract. You have to hear it. Name it. Feel when it enters the room. Notice how it talks. Because the inner critic doesn't always sound like shouting. Sometimes it's subtle. Polished. Reasonable. It disguises itself as pragmatism, responsibility, even ambition. It pretends it's keeping you safe, when what it's really doing is keeping you small.

Start by listening.

Pay attention to the tone of your inner monologue when something goes wrong. When you miss a deadline. Forget something. Make a social misstep. Procrastinate. Fail to show up the way you wanted to. Does the voice say, *That's okay, this is hard, you're still learning*? Or does it say, *What's wrong with you? You always do this. You're such a mess. Everyone else has figured this out by now?*

That's the critic.

Sometimes it sounds like you. But often, it isn't.

It might be your mother's voice. Or your father's. A coach. A teacher. A peer group. A boss. Someone who made you feel like love had conditions. Like belonging required performance. Like worth could be revoked.

The critic is rarely original. It repeats scripts. And those scripts get lodged in your nervous system, in your thought patterns, in your body. Not because you chose them, but because at some point, they felt necessary. Criticism, after all, can feel like control. And control feels safer than chaos.

But identifying the critic means slowing down enough to notice when it takes over—and what it's trying to prevent.

Ask yourself: When the voice shows up, what am I afraid will happen if I *don't* listen to it?

Will I be rejected? Exposed? Mocked? Will I lose respect? Be abandoned? Be seen as selfish, lazy, weak? The critic always has a fear underneath it. A belief about what might happen if you relax your vigilance. If you give yourself too much grace. If you soften.

And once you know what that fear is, you can begin to see the critic not as your enemy—but as a scared part of you, trying to keep you from pain.

This is especially true for people who grew up in emotionally inconsistent environments. Homes where praise and criticism were unpredictable. Where safety was tied to behavior. Where vulnerability wasn't met with care, but with withdrawal or punishment. In those settings, the child often internalizes the critical voice as a way to stay ahead of danger. *If I can catch the mistake before they do, maybe I won't get hurt.* That internalization becomes adaptive. But over time, it calcifies. And what once protected you starts to restrict you.

You don't have to hate the critic. But you do have to name it. Because until you do, it will feel like truth. Like reality. Like the voice of reason.

Sometimes it's relentless. *You'll never be enough. You're always too much. Why even try?* Other times it's more manipulative. *Don't get too confident. Don't rest. Don't let anyone see your flaws.* Either way, it's not guiding you—it's guarding you. Against risks that may no longer exist.

And if you're someone who prides yourself on self-awareness, this can get confusing. Because the critic can masquerade as introspection. It can convince you that it's being honest, objective, clear-eyed. But self-awareness without compassion is just self-monitoring. It's surveillance, not insight.

Real insight requires gentleness.

That's why identifying the critic is a compassionate act. You're not trying to exile it. You're trying to give it context. To say: I see you. I know where you came from. But I'm an adult now. I can handle complexity. I don't need to be policed to be valuable.

Start practicing this by externalizing the voice. Write it down when it speaks. Literally: "The critic is saying I'm behind and I'll never catch up." Then respond—not with argument, but with curiosity. *What fear is underneath this message? What part of me is being protected right now?*

The more you do this, the more separation you create. And in that separation, you start to recover your own voice—the one beneath the judgment. The one that knows the difference between truth and trauma. The one that can hold pain without making it into identity.

Because the critic isn't you. It's a strategy. And you get to outgrow it.

Parts Work and Protective Mechanisms

If you've ever felt like one part of you wants to rest while another part is screaming that you haven't earned it, you already understand parts work—whether you've heard the term or not.

Parts work, particularly in the Internal Family Systems (IFS) model developed by Richard Schwartz, rests on a deceptively simple truth: you are not a singular, unified self. You are a system. A constellation of sub-personalities, each with its own history, fears, needs, and strategies. These parts aren't flaws or symptoms. They're adaptive. And the inner critic is one of them.

IFS doesn't treat the inner critic as a mistake to be eradicated. It sees it as a protector. A part of you that learned, often early in life, that harsh self-monitoring could prevent rejection, punishment, or chaos. Maybe it developed in response to a volatile parent. Maybe it emerged during school, where excellence was rewarded and failure was punished. Maybe it came from culture, from religion, from being marginalized or underestimated. Wherever it came from, its job was the same: keep you safe by keeping you in line.

And it worked—for a while.

The critic helped you stay alert. Helped you preempt mistakes. Helped you survive in systems that required constant vigilance. But survival tools aren't always sustainable. What protected you as a child can become oppressive as an adult.

Because the critic doesn't evolve. It stays locked in the conditions it was built to manage. That's why it still treats every missed deadline like a crisis. Every mistake like a threat. It doesn't trust that you can repair, adapt, or be loved anyway. It doesn't trust that you're safe unless you're perfect. And it can't trust, because trust wasn't part of the system it was born into.

That's where parts work becomes transformative.

Instead of fighting the critic or trying to shut it down, IFS invites us to engage it—with curiosity, compassion, and boundaries. You begin by noticing when the critic takes over. Noticing what it says, what it feels like, where it lives in your body. Then you ask: what is this part afraid would happen if it stopped doing its job?

The answers are usually profound. *I'm afraid you'll get hurt. I'm afraid people will leave. I'm afraid you'll be exposed. I'm afraid you'll collapse.* That's when you realize: this part isn't trying to harm you. It's trying to prevent something it believes would be worse than the pain it causes. It's the emotional equivalent of a parent yelling at a child to look both ways. It's not kind. But it's trying to be protective.

And like many protectors, the critic often blocks access to more vulnerable parts of you—the ones carrying grief, loneliness, fear, shame. Those are your exiles. The parts that were too tender to be exposed, so they were buried. And the critic stands guard. If you're constantly self-monitoring, you don't have time to feel the sadness. Or the rage. Or the longing. You stay busy. You stay sharp. You stay ahead of pain.

But healing means letting the system soften.

That doesn't mean letting chaos reign. It means creating an internal relationship where each part is heard, respected, and cared for—without being allowed to dominate. You can thank the critic for its efforts without surrendering to its rule. You can acknowledge its fears without letting it dictate your decisions. You can say, *I know you're trying to keep me from being hurt—but I've got this now. I'm not a child anymore. I can take risks and recover. I don't need to earn my worth through punishment.*

This takes practice. Because the critic is often fused with your sense of identity. You may have been listening to it for so long that you don't know who you are without it. But you don't have to silence it all at once. You just have to create space. Enough space to ask: *Is this voice helping me? Is it telling the truth? What does it need in order to relax?*

That's where inner leadership begins.

You stop being ruled by whichever part is loudest. You start making space for the Self—the core of you that isn't a part at all, but the one who can hold them. The one who can listen, soothe, decide. The one who can say: I see you. I appreciate you. And I also know what's best for us now.

In that dynamic, the critic doesn't disappear. It transforms. It becomes a consultant, not a tyrant. It speaks, but it doesn't overrule. And sometimes, it quiets entirely—not because it was exiled, but because it finally feels safe enough to rest.

That's the heart of this work: understanding that your inner world is a living system. And systems don't heal through violence. They heal through relationship.

How We Mistake Criticism for Clarity

The inner critic doesn't always scream. Sometimes, it sounds calm. Logical. Even helpful. It tells you things like, *You need to be realistic. Don't get too comfortable. Don't fool yourself.* It presents itself as clarity—as hard truth, tough love, the only voice in your head willing to be honest with you. And that's what makes it so convincing.

But that voice isn't clarity. It's criticism wearing a mask.

Clarity helps you understand. Criticism reduces you to a flaw. Clarity creates movement. Criticism creates paralysis. Clarity sounds like: *Here's what didn't work, and here's what you can do next.* Criticism says: *You failed again. What's wrong with you?*

The difference isn't always in the words. It's in the energy. The emotional texture. The impact it has on your ability to move forward. Does the voice leave you with more possibility or less? Do you feel more human, more empowered, more capable—or more ashamed, diminished, defeated?

Most of us weren't taught to make that distinction. We were taught that being "hard on yourself" was a virtue. That if you didn't criticize yourself first, someone else would. That being self-aware meant being self-harsh. That rigorous self-scrutiny was the price of integrity.

But this belief system confuses punishment with growth.

Punishment doesn't build character. It builds compliance, avoidance, or collapse. It teaches you to fear error instead of learning from it. It trains you to equate mistakes with moral failure. And over time, it strips your ability to be honest with yourself—because if every misstep leads to shame, you stop telling yourself the truth.

This is why so many people confuse their inner critic with their conscience. They think the harsh voice is what keeps them accountable. That without it, they'd slide into laziness, selfishness, chaos. But what actually happens when the critic quiets down is that people begin to relate to themselves—not manage themselves. They shift from control to curiosity. From performance to presence.

And in that space, real clarity begins to emerge.

Clarity doesn't require you to be brutal. It asks you to be precise. Instead of global declarations like *I'm such a failure,* clarity says: *I didn't meet the deadline. Why? Was it avoidable? What conditions contributed to the delay? What do I need to adjust going forward?* It doesn't attack your identity—it analyzes your behavior in context. It sees patterns without turning them into destiny.

But getting to that level of internal dialogue takes practice—especially if you were raised in environments where self-criticism was modeled as strength. Maybe you had caregivers who narrated their own failures out loud, constantly diminishing themselves in front of you. Maybe you were praised for being "mature" because you internalized adult expectations early. Maybe you learned to preempt judgment by judging yourself first.

Those patterns stick. And they often intensify with achievement. High performers tend to become high self-monitors. The more success you have, the more pressure you feel to protect it. And the critic becomes your defense system—your inner auditor, constantly scanning for cracks, inefficiencies, risks.

But you can't grow while holding yourself hostage.

Real maturity doesn't mean being perpetually hard on yourself. It means being honest about what you need to change—without confusing imperfection with inadequacy. It means learning to distinguish between a constructive voice and a punitive one.

Here's one way to test it: after the voice speaks, ask yourself, *Do I feel more able to move forward—or more afraid to try again?*

If it's the latter, you're not hearing clarity. You're hearing fear in disguise.

Another test: try saying the exact same message to a friend you deeply respect. If the words feel cruel coming out of your mouth, they probably don't belong in your own head.

We don't become better people by being mean to ourselves. We become better by being in honest relationship with all of our parts—including the ones that are scared, messy, inconsistent. Clarity is what allows us to hold those parts without abandoning growth. It says: *You matter, even when you screw up. Let's figure out what needs to shift. Let's move forward, together.*

That's what makes space for integration. For wholeness. For the kind of accountability that's rooted in care, not control.

Because clarity doesn't demand perfection. It demands presence. And presence only becomes possible when you're no longer mistaking cruelty for truth.

Shifting From Inner Critic to Inner Witness

Once you've learned to identify the inner critic and understand its protective function, the next step is not to eliminate it, but to relate to it differently. That shift doesn't happen through force. It happens through the cultivation of a different internal role—one that doesn't attack, doesn't appease, and doesn't shut down. That role is the inner witness.

The inner witness is not neutral in the detached sense. It's warm. Present. Grounded. It doesn't try to correct your emotions. It doesn't tell you how you *should* be feeling. It simply notices. It observes without absorbing. It holds space without collapsing into the drama of the moment. And when you're living in a spiral of self-criticism, it's the part of you that can say: *Wait. Let me sit with this before I react.*

Unlike the inner critic, which jumps to conclusions and turns every mistake into a moral failure, the inner witness stays curious. It says, *Something in me is panicking right now. I wonder what this part is afraid of. I wonder what it needs.*

This isn't just a semantic distinction. It's a shift in the entire tone of your inner world.

Think about how many times you've gotten stuck in a feedback loop of shame. You miss a deadline. The critic flares up. You feel overwhelmed. You shut down. The critic calls you lazy. You spiral. But if you have access to the inner witness in that moment, everything softens. You still recognize what happened—but without the sharp edge of judgment. You still feel the weight of the mistake—but without collapsing under it.

And from that grounded place, you can actually respond.

This is the goal of trauma-informed healing: not to banish the parts of you that learned survival through harshness, but to put them in relationship with a steadier presence. A presence that says, *You don't have to manage this alone. I'm here now. I can help.*

Some people find this voice through therapy. Others through mindfulness or self-reflection or somatic work. But all of those paths involve the same movement: slowing down enough to notice the difference between the part that's reacting and the part that's observing. That's when you start to realize: I am not just the feelings I'm having. I am also the one who is aware of them.

And awareness creates choice.

When the critic says, *You're a mess,* the inner witness doesn't argue. It listens. And it replies, *I hear that part. I see how scared it is. But I'm not going to speak to myself that way anymore. That's not how we grow.*

This kind of self-talk isn't soft in the way the critic fears. It's firm. Boundaried. It doesn't allow emotional abuse just because it's coming from inside the house. It doesn't entertain cruelty as strategy. It sets a new tone. One that honors complexity without defaulting to collapse.

But this shift requires practice. Especially if the critic has been running the show for decades. At first, you might only notice the witness in hindsight. You'll reflect on a shame spiral and think, *I could have responded differently.* That's not failure. That's awareness building its muscles. Over time, the witness gets closer to the moment itself. Until eventually, it's there in real time—interrupting the critic, soothing the system, choosing a new response.

This is not about replacing the critic with a cheerleader. It's not about empty affirmations or denial. The witness doesn't lie to you. It tells the truth—but gently. It says, *You didn't follow through, and I wonder what got in the way.* It says, *That didn't go how you hoped, and that's okay.* It says, *We can look at this without losing ourselves.*

And the more you live from that place, the more trust you build. Not just with yourself, but within yourself. Your internal system begins to recalibrate. The critic learns that it doesn't need to scream to be heard. The wounded parts learn that they don't have to hide. You start to experience a kind of inner coherence—where all your parts have a place, but none of them are in charge alone.

That's what emotional safety looks like on the inside.

It's not a perfect system. The critic will still show up—especially under stress. But now, you'll recognize it. You'll know what it is. You'll remember that you're not it. And that recognition is freedom.

Because once you've built a relationship with the inner witness, you can weather almost anything. You can hear the old narratives and not collapse into them. You can feel the fear and keep moving. You can hold the tension of being imperfect and still valuable. And slowly, quietly, powerfully—you start to live from a different center.

One that doesn't require you to earn your way into being okay.

* * *

9

Why Healing Doesn't Feel Like Progress

Most of us are told that healing is a journey. But few of us are warned that it's also a dismantling—a quiet, interior unraveling that often looks nothing like progress at all. We picture recovery like a staircase or a sunrise: upward, steady, clear. But real healing doesn't come with applause. It doesn't hand out medals or momentous milestones. More often than not, it feels like you're going in circles. Like you're doing it wrong. Like the pain is getting worse instead of better.

That's because healing isn't linear. It's recursive. Subtle. Sometimes invisible. You don't always know when something shifts until long after it has. And when your mind is used to measuring worth through output, efficiency, or external validation, it's easy to look at your healing and assume it's not enough. You're still anxious. Still procrastinating. Still spiraling sometimes. You still overthink. Still react. Still get quiet when you wish you wouldn't.

But here's the part that most people don't say out loud: progress isn't always a feeling. Sometimes it's a decision. Sometimes it's a quiet "no" you say to an old pattern. Sometimes it's walking away from the same argument a little faster. Sometimes it's crying when you used to shut down. Sometimes it's recognizing the spiral mid-fall instead of after you've hit the ground.

This chapter is about that kind of progress.

The kind that doesn't sparkle. The kind that doesn't perform. The kind that doesn't always feel like success. We'll explore why emotional growth often masquerades as stagnation, why letting go of urgency is so hard in a world that praises productivity, and how healing can trigger an identity crisis when the roles you used to play no longer fit. We'll end by asking a difficult question: if healing doesn't offer external proof, how do we measure it at all?

Because the truth is: you may be getting better without ever feeling like you're getting "there." And that doesn't mean you're lost. It means you're living through a process that was never meant to be flashy. Only real.

Growth Without Gold Stars

It's easy to believe you're not improving when your progress doesn't look impressive.

Most systems of reward we grow up in—from school to work to relationships—teach us to recognize achievement through external markers. You get a grade. A trophy. A promotion. A compliment. Something tangible that tells you: you're doing well. You're on the right track. Keep going.

But healing doesn't hand out gold stars.

There's no certificate for setting a boundary that made you feel like a terrible person. No applause for spending the day in bed instead of dissociating through productivity. No award for resisting the urge to self-destruct, even if your brain told you nothing had changed. The progress you make in healing is often private, invisible, and emotionally uncomfortable. And without a clear way to track it, many people assume they're failing.

But that assumption is based on the wrong metric.

Healing isn't a performance. It's a return. A reorientation to yourself that doesn't always produce results others can see—or even results that *you* can feel right away. Sometimes it looks like the exact same reaction you've always had—only this time, you noticed it while it was happening. Sometimes it looks like relapse. Regression. Repeating the pattern, but with slightly more self-awareness. Sometimes it looks like nothing on the surface, while a storm of internal restructuring unfolds beneath.

And when that happens, it's easy to wonder: *Am I actually healing, or am I just stuck in the same place pretending it's growth?*

That doubt is normal. In fact, it's a sign that you're stepping out of the binary thinking that equates health with perfection. Progress with consistency. It means you're beginning to ask a deeper question—not *am I fixed yet,* but *what does it mean to relate to myself differently in the mess?*

Because real growth isn't just about what you do—it's about how you respond when you can't do what you hoped.

And that's hard to track. Especially in a culture obsessed with outcomes. You're taught to expect a straight line. To believe that every healthy change will feel good, affirming, empowering. But the truth is, many of the most important breakthroughs come wrapped in ambivalence. You feel heavier, not lighter. You cry more. You confront loss. You stop numbing. And all of it can make you question whether you're going backward.

But here's what's really happening: you're becoming honest.

You're facing what you used to suppress. Feeling what you used to deflect. Naming what you used to swallow. And that honesty is painful—but it's also foundational. You can't heal what you won't touch. You can't release what you haven't grieved. You can't integrate what you still believe is too shameful to acknowledge.

So if your growth feels disappointing, consider this: maybe you're not doing it wrong. Maybe you're finally doing it for real.

Maybe you're no longer chasing the feeling of progress—because you're beginning to understand that the absence of chaos isn't the same as wholeness. Maybe you're no longer trying to win at healing. Maybe you're learning how to live through it.

This shift is radical. It pulls you out of the external reward loop and into an internal recalibration. You stop asking, *Who sees this?* and start asking, *Do I feel more like myself?* You stop chasing signs of approval and start listening for signs of integrity. You stop comparing your process to someone else's highlight reel and start honoring the quiet work your nervous system is doing just to let you rest without guilt.

That doesn't mean it gets easy. But it does get truer.

Growth without gold stars teaches you to keep showing up without being seen. It teaches you to trust internal shifts before they translate into external change. It teaches you to let go of performance as a proxy for healing—and to begin building a relationship with yourself that isn't contingent on being impressive.

And if you're in that space right now—doing the work, unsure whether it "counts," wondering if you're making any real progress—know this: the fact that you're even asking those questions is evidence that something has shifted. People who are stuck in old patterns without reflection don't ask whether they're growing. They just repeat. The doubt you feel is the product of awareness. The tension is a sign of movement.

So no, you may not have gold stars. But you have something better.

You have presence. You have intention. You have the kind of honesty that can't be faked. And you're building a kind of resilience that doesn't need to be proven to be real.

Letting Go of Urgency

Healing is deeply uncomfortable for people who were raised in urgency. Not just the urgency of doing—but the urgency of becoming. Of getting better, quickly. Of fixing yourself fast enough that no one notices you're broken. Of arriving at a version of you that finally feels worthy, lovable, and safe.

Urgency is seductive. It promises relief. It tells you that if you just hurry up and get it right, you won't have to feel this way anymore. That the pain, the anxiety, the shame—all of it can be resolved through speed and efficiency. That healing is a sprint toward a destination called "finally okay."

But healing doesn't work like that. It's not efficient. It's not linear. And it refuses to meet the timelines set by your fear.

Letting go of urgency is one of the most difficult emotional tasks we face—especially in a culture that glorifies fast results and penalizes slow processes. In school, you're rewarded for early mastery. In jobs, you're expected to produce more in less time. In relationships, you're told to "get over it" before the discomfort becomes inconvenient for someone else. Even in therapy spaces, the pressure to demonstrate progress can override the actual work of being present with what hurts.

But urgency is rarely about the present. It's almost always about fear.

Fear that you're too late. Fear that you're falling behind. Fear that you'll be left out, left behind, left alone. And sometimes, that fear is a memory. A trauma echo. A residue from childhood, when approval was conditional and slowness was punished. Maybe you learned to be early to everything so no one could accuse you of being lazy. Maybe you learned to over-explain, over-apologize, over-function, so no one would think you were a burden. Maybe you became hyper-efficient as a way to manage someone else's volatility.

In those environments, urgency was a survival strategy. It helped you anticipate threat. Avoid shame. Stay useful enough to feel like you mattered. And when urgency works, it becomes your default. Even when the threat is gone.

Letting go of urgency means sitting in that space where nothing feels fixed—and resisting the urge to fix it.

It means noticing the impulse to speed up, and choosing instead to pause. To breathe. To stay. Not because you don't care. But because you're learning that care doesn't have to look like hustle. It can look like presence. Like staying with the feeling instead of running from it. Like allowing the wave to crest without forcing a resolution.

This doesn't mean complacency. It doesn't mean giving up or letting pain consume you. It means learning the difference between motion and movement. Between reaction and response. Between performing stability and building it slowly from the inside out.

There's a kind of grief that comes with this. A grief for the life you thought you'd have by now. The person you thought you'd be. The certainty you thought healing would give you. Letting go of urgency means letting go of the fantasy of emotional arrival—that someday, you'll be healed enough that life will stop hurting. That the right combination of insight and effort will finally unlock peace.

But healing doesn't remove difficulty. It changes your relationship to it.

And that's the work. Slowing down enough to feel what's underneath the panic. Sitting with the question, *What if there's nothing wrong with where I am right now?* That question alone can destabilize an entire system that's been built on proving, improving, racing. But it's also the question that opens the door to real integration.

Because urgency often keeps you in cycles. You set impossible standards. You fail to meet them. You shame yourself. You try harder. You burn out. And each time, you tell yourself it's because you didn't try hard enough, when in fact, it's because the pace itself is unsustainable.

Letting go of urgency means choosing sustainability over spectacle. Integrity over speed. It means letting your healing take the time it actually needs—not the time you think will make other people more comfortable.

This is slow work. Sometimes, achingly so. But slowness is not failure. It's fidelity—to the actual rhythms of your nervous system, your story, your becoming.

And the more you practice this pace, the more you realize: urgency was never about healing. It was about avoiding the feeling of being unworthy in the in-between. And when you learn to stay in the in-between without turning it into a problem to solve, something else emerges.

A different kind of wholeness. One that doesn't rely on timelines. One that doesn't expire when you struggle. One that waits with you, breath by breath, as you rebuild your relationship with time—not as a countdown, but as a container.

The Identity Crisis of Moving On

What no one tells you about healing is that it will change who you are—not just how you feel. And that's not always welcome news.

We often start healing because we're in pain. We want relief. We want answers. We want the parts of us that ache to stop aching. But healing isn't just about relief. It's about renovation. And sometimes, what gets stripped away isn't just the suffering. It's the identity that formed around it.

Maybe you were the fixer. The dependable one. The high achiever. The people pleaser. The one who never needed help. The one who made herself smaller to keep the peace. These roles might have earned you safety. Affection. Status. Predictability. But they were also costumes—adaptive, yes, but incomplete. When healing begins, those costumes start to fall apart. And what's underneath isn't always something you recognize.

That's where the identity crisis begins.

Healing asks: Who are you if you're not performing? Who are you when you're no longer driven by fear, validation, or survival patterns? Who are you without your pain as your primary story?

These aren't just abstract questions. They have real consequences. Because when you start to change internally, your external world doesn't always know what to do with you.

Relationships shift. Some deepen. Others fall away. People who were comfortable with the old version of you—compliant, self-sacrificing, anxious to please—may feel disrupted by the new version, even if that version is more honest. You might hear things like, *You've changed, You're being selfish,* or *You're not the same person I knew.*

And they're right. You're not.

But that doesn't mean you're doing it wrong. It means you're shedding an identity that was created in response to pain—not from the truth of who you are. And as that identity dissolves, there's a gap. A space between the old self and the emerging one. That space can feel disorienting, even terrifying. Because you're not just losing patterns—you're losing reference points.

You might wonder: If I'm not striving to be enough, what will motivate me? If I'm not constantly apologizing, will anyone still love me? If I stop over-functioning, who will I be?

This is where the grief comes in. Because even though your old identity was rooted in pain, it still gave you something. A sense of belonging. A sense of purpose. A role to play. And when that's gone, you have to rebuild—not just what you do, but how you understand yourself.

That rebuilding takes time. It requires you to get curious about who you are when no one's watching. What you want when you're not managing other people's expectations. What it feels like to act from desire instead of obligation.

And that's not always easy. Because for many people, pain wasn't just something that happened to them—it became part of how they made sense of the world. It gave their struggle a narrative arc. A kind of identity scaffolding. When that scaffolding falls, the rawness underneath can feel unbearable.

But that rawness is where your real self begins.

The self that isn't driven by pathology or performance. The self that doesn't need to earn rest or prove resilience. The self that doesn't fit neatly into the old story—but also doesn't need to.

The key is to stay present in the disorientation. To allow yourself to feel unmoored without rushing to define the new version of you. To hold the ambiguity. To know that just because you don't recognize yourself yet doesn't mean you're lost. It means you're in motion. It means the story is still unfolding.

And slowly, you begin to fill in the outlines of a self that isn't reacting to fear—but responding to life. A self who can tolerate contradiction. Who can honor the past without being beholden to it. Who doesn't need to be perfect to be whole.

That's the real identity work of healing. Not trading one costume for another, but dismantling the need for a costume at all. Living without armor. Letting people see you, not just your coping strategies. And learning, moment by moment, to trust that who you are becoming is not a problem to solve—but a truth to uncover.

How to Measure the Unmeasurable

When progress can't be tracked, the mind panics. It wants data. Markers. Something concrete to prove that the effort has been worth it. That you're not just floundering in emotional quicksand. That all the hard conversations, the tears, the awkward boundaries, the quiet courage—it all adds up to something.

But emotional growth rarely comes with metrics.

You don't get a badge when you stop reacting the way you used to. No monthly report tells you your inner child felt 12% safer this week. No spreadsheet can capture how it felt to sit with discomfort without abandoning yourself. And that makes healing feel slippery. If you can't measure it, how can you trust it's real?

The problem isn't that growth is unmeasurable. It's that we've been taught to measure the wrong things.

We've learned to track productivity, not presence. Output, not integration. Results, not regulation. But healing lives in the unmeasurable spaces—the microshifts in your nervous system, the pauses that used to be filled with panic, the tiny decisions to choose alignment over approval. The world may not see those changes. But you do. If you know what to look for.

So how do you measure healing?

You start by changing the lens. Instead of asking, *What did I accomplish today?*, ask *How did I relate to myself?* Were you gentler when you made a mistake? Did you notice the shame voice and breathe instead of spiraling? Did you reach out for connection before your brain convinced you it was unsafe? These moments are seismic—even if no one claps.

Measure your capacity to stay in the room with your feelings.

Measure how often you catch the old patterns before they carry you away.

Measure how quickly you return to center—not whether you avoid chaos altogether, but how you come back from it.

Measure the fact that you no longer believe every cruel thing your inner critic says without question.

Measure the space between the trigger and your reaction. That's progress.

Measure the fact that you know what a trigger *is* now. That you can name your nervous system states. That you've learned to distinguish discomfort from danger.

Measure the relationships you've let go of because they cost your peace. Measure the ones you've repaired because you learned how to speak the truth without collapsing.

Measure how many times you've honored your needs without needing permission. How many times you've let go of urgency. How many days you rested without earning it.

These are the metrics that matter. But they're internal. Which means no one else may ever notice them. And that's what makes this work so disorienting. You're changing everything about how you live—and it looks like nothing.

But invisibility doesn't mean it's not real.

Some of the most radical healing happens in silence. When no one sees it. When no one praises it. When it's just you, deciding to do something differently than the way you were trained. That's a revolution. Even if it feels mundane.

You'll still have days when you wonder if you're making progress. That's okay. The mind wants certainty. But healing lives in relationship—not in resolution. It's not something you finish. It's something you learn to live with. To engage with. To return to.

So on the days you feel stuck, ask better questions. Not *Am I healed yet?* but *Did I show up honestly today?* Not *Why am I still struggling?* but *What part of me is asking for care?* Not *When will this be over?* but *What's emerging that I've never let myself feel before?*

That's how you measure what can't be measured.

Not by tracking perfection, but by witnessing presence. Not by eliminating all pain, but by expanding your capacity to hold it. Not by becoming someone new, but by reclaiming the parts of you that were always there—just waiting for the noise to quiet enough to be heard.

That's the real proof. And it was never meant to be flashy. Only real.

* * *

10

A Different Kind of Enough

There comes a moment in nearly every healing journey when you ask a quieter question—not how to succeed, or how to win, or even how to feel better—but how to live. Not perform. Not perfect. Just live. In a way that feels honest. Whole. Grounded. In a way that isn't tethered to endless evaluation.

That moment usually comes after you've tried everything else.

You've chased success. You've rewritten yourself a dozen times. You've optimized your schedule, rebranded your identity, pursued therapy, bought the books, followed the experts, meditated and journaled and processed and read every listicle on how to fix yourself. And still—somewhere beneath it all—you're tired. Not because you haven't grown. But because you've realized the finish line keeps moving.

The goalposts of "being okay" are never where they said they'd be.

You get the degree, and then you need the next one. You reach the goal weight, and then the mirror changes. You publish the book, launch the thing, impress the crowd—and still, the satisfaction is fleeting. The metrics shift. The expectations double. Enough never stays enough for long.

This chapter is about breaking that spell.

Not by pretending you don't care. But by choosing to live by a different standard—one that isn't defined by constant pursuit. One that doesn't require you to earn your rest. One that values being over becoming.

We'll begin by rethinking the entire framework of success—not as arrival, but as alignment. Then we'll explore the idea of worth that doesn't need accomplishment to justify itself. We'll talk about agency, rest, and the quiet revolution of emotional sovereignty—what it means to live in your own life without apology. And finally, we'll imagine what it looks like to move through the world rooted in a felt sense of enough-ness, even when nothing around you validates it.

Because if healing is going to mean anything, it has to lead somewhere other than perfection.

Maybe it leads to this: not the finish line, but the quiet knowing that you're allowed to be exactly where you are. That you don't have to climb your way into worthiness. That you were never broken. Only buried.

Rethinking Success and Arrival

Most of us were raised on a story that told us success was a place. A destination. A final point of arrival where doubt disappears, pain quiets, and self-worth becomes stable and undeniable. Get there, and you'll feel whole. Get there, and life will finally make sense.

It's a comforting myth. And a dangerous one.

Because the truth is: there is no finish line. Not in healing. Not in becoming. Not in whatever version of "getting it together" you've been holding onto for years. What we think of as arrival is often just a moment of relief—followed quickly by a new set of expectations. A new goal to chase. A new version of yourself to live up to.

Success, as we've been taught to define it, is rarely a landing. It's a moving target. And that target is shaped by culture, capitalism, trauma, and legacy. It's shaped by the belief that you are only as valuable as your performance. That your worth must be proven. That there is some ultimate form of yourself out there waiting to be unlocked through effort, optimization, and hustle.

But what if that's the wrong frame entirely?

What if success isn't a summit, but a state of congruence—between your values, your choices, and your presence?

What if arrival isn't about achieving peace, but about no longer needing perfection to feel it?

These questions unsettle the systems we've built our identities on. They force us to look at the ways we've confused visibility with value, output with purpose, and external validation with internal truth.

Because the culture will never stop selling you the idea that more is the answer. That if you just get the next thing—money, recognition, love, discipline, insight—you'll finally feel secure. But enough doesn't come from addition. It comes from excavation. From peeling back every inherited definition of worth that taught you to fear stillness.

And when you stop running, you realize: you were never chasing success. You were chasing safety.

That's what makes this shift so emotionally charged. Redefining success means redefining safety. Redefining what it means to be okay. Redefining the criteria by which you measure your right to rest, to love, to exist in a body without apology.

It's terrifying to let go of the ladder when you've been taught it's the only thing holding you up. But the ladder was never stable. It was built on scarcity—on the idea that you are always behind, always lacking, always needing to do more to deserve what should have never been conditional in the first place.

So what replaces it?

Not passivity. Not resignation. Not pretending ambition doesn't matter. What replaces it is intention. Discernment. A slower kind of striving, rooted in care rather than fear. You can still build. Still reach. Still create. But you're no longer doing it to outrun shame. You're doing it because it aligns with who you are when no one's watching.

That's the redefinition.

Success becomes about coherence. Integrity. The quiet satisfaction of living in rhythm with your values, even when no one applauds. Arrival becomes about presence—being in your life, as it is, without the constant need to upgrade or escape it.

And perhaps most importantly, worth becomes something you stop trying to earn—and start remembering.

Because you were never meant to be in a race. You were meant to be in a relationship—with yourself, with your body, with the world. And relationships are not won. They are tended.

Belonging Without Earning

The human need to belong is not a luxury. It's survival. From the moment we're born, we're wired to seek connection—emotional warmth, acceptance, attunement. And in a perfect world, that belonging would be unconditional. We'd be held in love simply because we exist. We'd learn, from the beginning, that our place in the world does not require performance.

But most of us don't live in that world.

Instead, we learn early that love has rules. That presence must be earned. That the price of belonging is often self-abandonment. You behave a certain way. You shrink what's too big. You amplify what's rewarded. You adjust your tone, your body, your personality—until the real you becomes secondary to the version that's safest to present.

That's how many of us learn to survive. But it's also how we learn the false equation: worth = utility.

In families where love was conditional, this might have looked like praise only when you excelled. Or affection only when you were compliant. Maybe your needs were too much, so you learned to become low-maintenance. Maybe your emotions were inconvenient, so you learned to numb. Somewhere along the way, you internalized the belief that you were acceptable only when you were easy to digest.

The pain of that lesson doesn't vanish with age. It embeds itself in how you work, how you love, how you show up. You over-function. You over-explain. You preemptively adjust to avoid rejection. And it feels normal—because it's familiar.

But it's not belonging. It's appeasement.

Belonging, in its truest form, cannot be earned. The moment you have to perform for it, you're no longer in a relationship—you're in a transaction. And the nervous system knows the difference. You feel it in your stomach. In your jaw. In the way your body braces when you enter a room, hoping you're not "too much" again.

The work of healing here is not to become more likable. It's to unlearn the belief that likability is your currency.

That's where the psychology of unconditional worth begins. Not with self-esteem boosts or empty affirmations—but with the radical idea that you do not need to justify your presence. That your needs are not a nuisance. That your softness is not a flaw. That your dignity is not contingent on being palatable.

This reorientation doesn't happen all at once. It starts with small acts of defiance. Saying no when you'd usually say yes. Letting yourself be seen when you're not polished. Choosing rest over performance. Saying what you actually feel, even if it shakes. Each of these is a quiet rebellion against the lie that your value depends on usefulness.

It also means examining the relationships in your life. Who loves the version of you that performs? Who stays when you disappoint? Who withholds when you're human? These are hard questions. But they're clarifying. Because belonging without earning requires space to be fallible, to be messy, to be real.

And yes, this comes with risk. Some people won't stay when you stop performing. Some dynamics will shift when you stop managing everyone else's comfort. But the loss of performative relationships makes room for authentic ones. The ones where you don't have to contort. Where your full self is not only tolerated—but welcomed.

This isn't about being celebrated all the time. It's about not being punished for showing up as you are.

Unconditional worth doesn't mean you never grow or stretch. It means growth is no longer a prerequisite for love. You get to evolve because you want to—not because you fear you'll be left behind if you don't.

And as you practice this shift, something inside softens. The anxious scanning fades. The people-pleasing quiets. You begin to inhabit yourself—not as a brand or a role—but as a person. Fully human. Irrevocably worthy.

Not someday. Not once you've healed enough. But now.

Agency, Rest, and Emotional Sovereignty

One of the clearest signs that healing is taking root is the reclamation of choice. Not just the freedom to choose, but the internal permission to believe that your choices matter. That your life is yours to live. That your time is not automatically up for negotiation. That your energy is not everyone else's to spend.

This is what emotional sovereignty means. And for many people, it's a foreign language.

If you were taught to be adaptable, accommodating, or agreeable as a means of survival, then autonomy can feel threatening. Rest can feel lazy. Saying no can feel like betrayal. And choosing for yourself—without justification or apology—can feel selfish, or even dangerous.

That's because many of us learned agency as rebellion, not as a right.

You weren't allowed to ask questions. You were called difficult when you had boundaries. You were told that your opinions were disrespectful. So you learned to override your own signals. You internalized the belief that someone else's comfort was more important than your truth. You became fluent in silence. You learned to read a room before you read yourself.

That skill—hyper-attunement to others—might have kept you safe. But it cost you sovereignty.

Reclaiming it starts slowly. It doesn't require becoming loud or aggressive or permanently unbothered. It requires honesty. A quiet checking-in. Do I actually want this? Do I have the capacity for this? Am I saying yes to stay safe, or because it aligns with who I am?

That pause is a radical act. Especially in a culture that conflates agency with arrogance, and rest with weakness.

Let's talk about rest.

Real rest is not just about sleeping more or going on vacation. It's about choosing not to be in performance mode every waking minute. It's about stepping out of hypervigilance. It's about letting yourself be unproductive without spiraling into guilt or shame.

And for many, rest is terrifying.

Because rest invites you to feel. And what surfaces in stillness can be overwhelming—especially when you've used motion, achievement, or caretaking as distractions. In this way, rest isn't passive. It's confrontational. It forces you to meet yourself without the buffer of busyness.

But it's also where clarity begins.

When you're no longer chasing someone else's idea of worth, you begin to hear your own voice again. And that voice is the foundation of sovereignty.

Emotional sovereignty is not detachment. It's not being unaffected or impervious. It's knowing where you end and someone else begins. It's taking full ownership of your reactions without absorbing the responsibility for everyone else's. It's being rooted enough in your own internal compass that external noise doesn't automatically reroute your sense of direction.

This kind of sovereignty makes space for rest—not just as a recovery tactic, but as a right. It makes space for joy that isn't conditional. For no's that don't need explanations. For a life that's designed around who you are, not just what others expect from you.

The most powerful part of this work is often the quietest: not reacting, not rushing, not apologizing for simply being in your own life with both feet planted.

And yes, there will be discomfort. There will be resistance—internal and external. People may not know what to do with your new clarity. That's okay. Let them adjust. Your job is not to stay digestible. It's to stay truthful.

And the more you practice agency and rest without self-betrayal, the more your nervous system learns a new baseline—where peace isn't something to earn, but something you return to.

That is sovereignty. Not domination. Not avoidance. Not certainty. Just the steady, internal knowing: *I belong to myself.*

Living Outside the Metrics

At some point, if you're lucky—and willing—your healing will take you beyond the realm of measurement. Beyond productivity logs, beyond self-improvement goals, beyond the impulse to track and tally your life like it's a performance review.

This doesn't mean abandoning growth. It means releasing the tyranny of measurement as your primary orientation to worth.

Most of us are taught from an early age to think in metrics. Grades. Gold stars. Steps walked. Words written. Calories burned. Posts liked. Followers gained. It's the logic of quantification: prove your value by making it visible, countable, comparable.

In that world, the question becomes not *how are you?* but *how well are you doing at being a person?*

And "well" is defined by output.

Even healing—an internal, nonlinear, deeply personal process—gets absorbed into the metric machine. How many sessions have you done? What milestones have you hit? Are you more regulated? Are you better yet?

But wholeness doesn't live in a graph. And enoughness can't be measured in milestones.

Living outside the metrics means refusing to let numbers narrate your life. It means dropping the illusion that anything truly meaningful about you can be tallied or compared. It means recognizing that the most sacred shifts often have no visible footprint. No audience. No trophy.

This shift can feel disorienting. If you're used to tracking your value by how much you produce or achieve, then stopping that tracking feels like stepping into fog. What now? Who am I without my stats?

The answer isn't immediate. But it's real.

You start noticing moments that were previously invisible. The exhale when you don't respond to the old trigger. The choice to pause instead of push. The fact that your joy today isn't performative. That you're not planning how to share it. That it belongs to you alone.

Living outside the metrics is about finding a different pulse. One that doesn't depend on external rhythm or validation. It's about aligning your life with internal signals: Does this nourish me? Am I being honest? Is this rooted in care?

That orientation changes everything.

Suddenly, rest is no longer time wasted. Presence is no longer incidental.

Play isn't frivolous—it's restorative. And solitude isn't a gap in the calendar—it's a reclamation of space.

Of course, the world will still try to measure you. Capitalism doesn't reward stillness. Social media doesn't favor nuance. Institutions rarely make room for slow, quiet unfolding. But you don't have to internalize their metrics as truth.

You can choose to measure your life differently.

In how much peace you feel when you wake up. In how little you explain yourself to people who don't ask good questions. In how easily you can say no without shame. In how often you feel rooted, rather than scattered. In the number of times a day you return to yourself, gently, instead of running away.

These aren't things you post. They don't show up on your resume. But they are the markers of a life grounded in enoughness.

And that's the kind of enough we're building here.

Not performative enough. Not comparative enough. Not temporary, fragile, audience-dependent enough.

But a different kind.

The kind that says: I am here. I am real. I don't need to earn air. I don't need to upgrade my humanity. I am already someone to return to.

Not because I've won at healing. But because I've stopped trying to win at all.

That's where we end. Not with a celebration of what you've achieved—but with a quiet honoring of what you've reclaimed.

Your pace. Your presence. Your personhood.

That's enough. That's always been enough.

* * *

You Weren't Meant to Live in Constant Evaluation

There's a certain kind of exhaustion that doesn't come from overwork—it comes from over-monitoring. From carrying the weight of constant self-surveillance. From evaluating your every decision, word, habit, and feeling through the lens of "Am I doing this right?"

It's a kind of internal bureaucracy. A committee of voices watching, judging, tallying. You wake up and assess your productivity potential for the day. You scroll through other people's lives and quietly compare. You think about how you sounded in yesterday's meeting. You reword texts before sending them. You do mental accounting every hour: Was I kind enough? Did I rest too long? Was I too much? Was I enough?

This book has not been about solving that entirely. Because it's not a problem to fix—it's a culture to unlearn. A way of being that many of us absorbed without consent. It's in our schools, our workplaces, our families, our relationships, our phones. It's everywhere.

But we don't have to internalize it.

You weren't meant to live in constant evaluation. You weren't meant to measure your worth in units of usefulness. You weren't built to be optimized—you were built to be. And that means feeling, changing, messing up, growing slowly, grieving what's gone, and waking up most mornings unsure of what exactly you're doing—but doing it anyway, because you're alive and trying.

If you feel tired, it's not because you're broken. It's because the metrics by which you've been asked to prove yourself were never designed to hold the full complexity of a human life. The pressure to perform a coherent, upwardly mobile, impressive version of yourself is a performance that extracts far more than it gives.

This book has tried to name what gets lost in that performance: the inner life.

Not the curated one. The real one. The emotional undercurrents. The invisible decisions. The quiet endurance of people who feel like they're failing—not because they're inadequate, but because they're human in a culture that doesn't make room for that.

So much of our suffering stems from the illusion that we're supposed to be different by now.

That we should've arrived already. That we should've gotten over it. That we should've caught up, figured it out, healed better, grown faster. That belief is not neutral. It's corrosive. It turns ordinary human experiences—grief, exhaustion, uncertainty—into evidence of personal defect.

But here's the shift: what if none of it meant you were failing?

What if being disoriented, emotional, or overwhelmed wasn't a flaw in the system—but a clue that you were still awake inside it?

What if all the places you feel behind are actually places where the world has made impossible demands, and your soul has refused to comply?

That's not failure. That's fidelity. To yourself. To your limits. To your history. To your pace.

There are no final steps here. No twelve-point plan. No trick to hack your nervous system into eternal peace. Just a different way of seeing.

And what you see, when you step back from the metrics, is that much of what you believed was personal inadequacy was actually cultural gaslighting.

You weren't lazy. You were burned out. You weren't scattered. You were surviving. You weren't unmotivated. You were misaligned. You weren't "behind." You were just not on someone else's imaginary timeline.

And the truth is, you were never behind in the first place. You were just living.

Sometimes slowly. Sometimes chaotically. Sometimes in ways that didn't look good from the outside. But you were living, and growing, and making choices in the best way you could, with the tools you had, in systems that often made no sense.

What we call inadequacy is often the mismatch between who we are and who we were told we should be.

This book has tried to bring that into focus. Not to give you a new script, but to clear the noise so you can hear your own.

Because the real work isn't about becoming a better version of yourself. It's about becoming less attached to the idea that there was ever something wrong with who you are right now.

To be fully alive is not to be perfectly optimized. It's to have access to your own presence, even when things are unfinished. It's to hold space for your contradictions. To stop negotiating with your self-worth. To live in the body you have, in the moment you're in, without always needing to explain it.

That might mean crying at odd hours. Or feeling proud of yourself for resting. Or noticing that you're no longer panicking about things that used to send you into a spiral. It might mean being bored, or unfollowing people who make you feel less than, or finally telling someone that what they said ten years ago actually hurt.

It might mean doing nothing "impressive" for a while.

It might mean making peace with the fact that healing doesn't always feel good. That it doesn't always make sense. That there's no gold star for learning how to soothe your own nervous system at 2 a.m. when no one else is there.

But that is the work.

The real, invisible, unmeasured, uncelebrated work of becoming a person who lives in their life, not outside of it.

And that life doesn't need to be remarkable. It needs to be yours.

So if you're still here—reading, wondering, breathing—know this: You are not the sum of your progress. You are not your metrics. You are not your likes, your habits, your past, or your pace.

You are a person. A whole one. Even when you don't feel like it.

And that's enough.

It always was.

* * *

About the Author

RJ Starr is an Academic Psychologist, Professor, and Author whose work explores the emotional and existential challenges at the heart of human life—how we make meaning, shoulder responsibility, and stay grounded in times of uncertainty. Known for a voice that is both thought-provoking and deeply accessible, he invites readers into greater self-awareness, emotional clarity, and purpose. When not teaching or writing, he reflects on the inner lives we carry and shares his insights with audiences around the world.

You can connect with me on:

https://profrjstarr.com

www.ingramcontent.com/pod-product-compliance
Lightning Source LLC
LaVergne TN
LVHW022059200926
848481LV00003B/985